The Shaver Mystery Discussion On Long John Nebel PartyLine, 1958
Part I

Kenneth Arnold

SAUCERIAN PUBLISHER

ISBN: 9798590129195

ISBN-13: 9798590129195

GTIN-14 : 09798590129195

© 2021, Saucerian Publisher

Long John Nebel

INDEX

Prologue

"Long John Nebel (born John Zimmerman; June 11, 1911 – April 10, 1978) was an influential New York City talk radio show host.

From the mid-1950s until his death in 1978, Nebel was a hugely popular all-night radio host, with millions of regular listeners and what Donald Bain described as "a fanatically loyal following" to his syndicated program, which dealt mainly with anomalous phenomena, UFOs, and other offbeat topics.

Nebel's program gave the impression of being freewheeling and unpredictable, prone to sidetracks and digressions; very different from the precise, mannered approach of most contemporary radio. There were occasional heated arguments—rather mild when compared to the conflict on more recent programs such as the Jerry Springer Show, but such open conflict in any media was quite startling in the 1950s and 1960s.

Nebel, along with his regular guests and panelists, would interview various personalities and claimants (such as psychic Kuda Bux), and take occasional telephone calls from listeners in the New York area. He would also interview novelists and discuss their books in detail. He was surprised on one occasion by novelist Iris Murdoch's response that she was a frequent listener and had modeled one of her characters after one of his guests.

Nebel's approach was unique: talk radio per se did not yet exist as it would in later decades, and Nebel was navigating largely uncharted territory. Sometimes, Nebel entered the discussions, other times he described himself as a "moderator" and allowed his guests to have spirited debates, commenting only occasionally to guide the debate, or to announce station breaks.

It was not uncommon for Nebel to disappear for 20 minutes or more around 3:00 am and leave his panel of frequent guests to run the show without him. Nebel usually invited callers during the last two hours of the program (from about 3:00 to 5:00 am); up to 40,000 people might try to telephone during this period.

Nebel was perhaps best described as a curious skeptic with respect to the reality of paranormal topics; he frequently characterized himself as a "non-believer". Regarding the claims of the many contactees he interviewed, Nebel stated: "I don't buy any of it." He also noted that he was intrigued by some UFO reports, but did not have any firm conclusions or explanations. Some critics attacked Nebel for allowing crackpots free rein on the program, but he responded by saying his was not a traditional news or investigative journalism show, and that it was up to listeners to determine the validity of any guest's claims.

Nebel often asked pointed questions of his guests when he saw logical fallacies or inconsistencies in their stories. He did not suffer fools gladly, unless the fool was exceptionally entertaining. Still, he was rather sympathetic in at least offering guests a forum to state their claims.

When programs dealt with health and exercise, Nebel was fond of saying: "I am a lover, not an athlete." He also popularized the expression "wack-a-ding-hoi" for an idea or guest he believed was a little "crazy". When asked why his television show was no longer on the air, Nebel would respond that he was not good-looking enough to be on television. His friendly, good-humored approach was one of the great reasons for his popularity.

Flying saucers were in the news regularly in the mid-1950s, and were a frequent topic on Nebel's show. Guests related to this subject included retired Marine Corps Major Donald Keyhoe, contactees George Adamski and George Van Tassel, and skeptics like Arthur C. Clarke and Lester del Rey. Nebel discussed the so-called Shaver Mystery, the Flatwoods monster, the Nazca Lines, and many other uncommon subjects.

Nebel gave a forum to Otis T. Carr, an Oklahoman who claimed to have discovered the secret of flying saucer propulsion, by studying the works of Nikola Tesla. With some of his regular panelists, Nebel journeyed to Oklahoma City for the unveiling of Carr's saucer. Carr was later convicted of fraud and jailed after he took several hundred thousand dollars from investors, and never produced his prototype.

Nebel was not above a few pranks, all in the name of showmanship and ratings: on one occasion, for example, he colluded with a friend to offer testimony supporting a guest's claims of astral projection.

Nebel spent weeks on his show developing a tale for his audience that the Empire State Building was rotated on giant ball bearings in the wee hours of the morning. At first Nebel said the motion was almost imperceptible. As the prank developed over time, Nebel began telling callers that if they visited the Empire State Building very late at night, they would find the shops at ground level had switched location to the block around the corner.

Nebel also was fond of telling his audience that the finest candle wicks were grown on "wick farms" located in the Midwest.

The fact that Nebel's second wife, Candy Jones claimed to have been the subject of CIA experiments in mind-control was discounted as a prank by those who pointed out his history of promoting hoaxes. Nebel, on the other hand, said that he believed what Jones had revealed to him under hypnosis, and never believed that her story was false in any way.

Although long plagued with heart disease, he was diagnosed with prostate cancer in 1971. Nebel sought various treatments, but by the mid-1970s, he was in very poor health. He continued broadcasting, however, usually six nights per week, with Candy Jones as his co-host. Nebel died in 1978 and his Mutual network slot was taken over by Larry King. His show on WOR, called "Partyline", was handed to James Randi, skeptic and frequent guest on Nebel's show over the years. "

In March, 1958, John Long Nebel, with three guests: Augie Robertson, Dominick Lucchesi & Ben Isquith discussed the Shaver Mystery. This is fascinating bit of UFO / Paranormal History. In this conversation, we can listen John Long talks about the Shaver Mystery. The discussion includes anecdotes about a young Harlan Ellison, and of *The Shaver Mystery* in general, as well as on the stories of George Adamksi. Also, Gray Barker, Albert K. Bender's "Men In Black" incident, Murray Island incident, Interplanetary travel, 2nd Washington sighting are discussed.

This conversation was recorded at that time, and the audio quality is not up to modern standards. The noise involved make sometimes hard to understand. However, most of the time it is understandable. As a result, we decided to publish this interview as a text. Because the audio quality, it was not possible to publish this conversation as a dialogue.

Saucerian Publisher was founded with the mission of promoting books in Flying Saucers, Paranormal, and the Occult. Our vision is to preserve the legacy of literary history by reprint editions of books which have already been exhausted or are difficult to obtain. Our goal is to help readers, educators and researchers by bringing back original publications that are difficult to find at reasonable price, while preserving the legacy of universal knowledge. This book is an authentic reproduction of the original Long John Nebel's radio show from 1958 (topic: The Shaver Mystery) as printed text. **IMPORTANT.** Despite the fact that we have attempted to accurately maintain the integrity of the original conversation, the present transcription may have minor errors beyond our control like: missing parts and the spelling of correct words. Because this book is culturally important, we have made available as part of our commitment to protect, preserve and promote knowledge in the world. This material was originally broadcasted in 1958.

At the end of the transcrip of the radio broadcast, we prepared a dictionary of some terms used during the discussion , followed by some news paper articles on the Shaver Mystery. Also, we have included tree original works published by Richard S. Shaver in *The* HIDDEN WORLD, Spring, 1961 with the aim to shed some lights on Nebel's discussion on the Shaver Mystery.

These articles are: *THE ANCIENT ALPHABET, A DICTIONARY OF THE MANTONG LANGUAGE & WHY THE CAVES ARE SECRET.*

Editor
Saucerian Publisher, 2021

Transcript of The Shaver Mystery Discussion On Long John Nebel PartyLine, 1958 Part I

Shaver's devil, a Dero

[00:00:29.640]

We're going to be talking this morning to a number of people, Augie Roberts is with us, **Dominick Lucchesi**. I understand that Jonah may join us for a period of time and then with the cybernetician. And we've had so many letters and cards from people telling us that they'd like to know more about the Deros, some people believe in **Deros,** some people don't. We've had people that tell us it's science fiction. Other people tell us that this is true.

[00:01:01.570]

I don't know. Frankly, I'm sort of a non-believer, but we'll find out this morning or at least we'll ask a number of questions. And I hope that we'll be able to get a number of answers. And if I'm correct, I think that the beginning of the famous Deros story or the **Shaver Mystery** was actually this was started by Ray Palmer. Its no true?. Yes, it was started while Ray Palmer was the editor of *Amazing Stories*. **Ray Palmer** was the editor of *Amazing Stories* for 12 years.

[00:01:39.450]

And during this time, Palmer did run the series, which were written by Richard S. Shaver, which Palmer admitted he penned in order to make it more interesting for the readers of *Amazing Stories*. Now, that original story, which really created the whole Shaver Mystery, so to speak, was a history called: *I remember Lemuria,*

THE FALL OF LEMURIA
by RICHARD S. SHAVER

For ages man has had memories of dead civilizations so vague that he has called them myths. Here is a story which suggests that not only were there such races, but that survivors still inhabit the earth!

which was written in nineteen forty five, and then right after that story hit the stands, and people began to read the magazine, and began, it began to get circulated around.

[00:02:21.420]

And the next month, 50,000 letters were received by W. B. Ziff, who was the publisher at the time, and that was after the first printing of the story, John. Now, actually Shaver wrote these thought records as he called later on, and I'll explain just how that came about. And trying to figure how can you write a thought record? Well, Shaver claimed that he was receiving messages. So I thought that when you set a record, I was thinking of a disc turntable.

[00:02:58.060]

Yes, maybe something like that, John. Actually, we don't know just what these mechanisms in the cabins report say the queen, but actually the history of this race of beings who resided on the earth twenty thousand years ago was on a thought record, and been transmitted by a mechanism, in one of the caverns. And when I say that, I have to go into details about what was Shaver in the cavern where he saw this equipment, a little later on, he claims to have had some type of another time rushing you, you know, more or less if you continue, I'm sure, because we'd have to get down to the bottom of this.

[00:03:39.480]

He was working as the botton of the cavern. I might to Well, I'd like to believe it. And I think I know just about how to go about it. But I wouldn't be all right. Wouldn't be proper to say that because many people could get into great danger attempting to enter the caverns. Now, Shaver worked as a welder for a shipyard. And he claimed that these thought records were being received by him while he was welding, not whether the welding or it had anything to do with the pick up of these records which were transmitted through the earth's shells, so to speak, from the caverns, I don't know.

[00:04:22.320]

But he claimed that these messages he began to hear these voices sort of sort of a super E.S.P. Now, of course, E.S.P. advanced by a welder, isn't credited as much as when it's advanced by someone like mine or some more qualified individual. But I think that maybe, it could be the possibility exists that Shaver actually was receiving some type of information by E.S.P. I don't know. And yet during as the mystery unfolded, during the period of years that *Amazing Stories* published, that there were some things that Shaver said and stated and predicted, more or less, which actually seemed as though he was receiving some form of information from some other source, so to speak.

[00:05:19.530]

Because from what I can gather from Ray himself, Ray Palmer, is that Palmer claims that Shaver used to send these manuscripts into

Glorious Yeave, Elder God, led us into battle against the fortress of Old Zelt

him and he would have to edit. And these manuscripts were written on the backs of envelopes, scrap paper. In other words, they were they weren't in proper form for submission to any publication. What was their reason for this? Was Mr Shaver a poor man and couldn't afford? I don't think so, John. I think that he was just a little odd, we may say, in this way of writing.

[00:05:54.270]

He probably wrote when he received these so-called messages, he would find an envelope in his pocket, more or less the way it appeared, not anything. Let's put it this way. That's the way Shaver made it appear anyway. And I don't know whether he did it because he didn't have paper. He couldn't afford it. But that is the way Palmer claims he used to receive these manuscripts.Now, Shaver sent these manuscripts and they condensed form and he sent them into *Amazing Stories* as true.

[00:06:24.600]

Now, *Amazing Stories* up to that time. Ever print a non-fiction story?. No, strangely enough, John, before *I remember Lemuria* was published in *Amazing Stories*, Shaver, I believe, did a small sort of a two page deal which dealt with an alphabet which he claimed to have received or had possession of, Shaver should receive this alphabet, and that was printed in nineteen forty three, from what I hear, which was before the story *I remember Lemuria* .

[00:07:01.500]

And according to Palmer, after the story, *I remember Lemuria* was published, these 50,000 letters, I means it's very difficult to believe, of course, but grandma claims that they are almost the only 50,000 letters or more of us that we make very positive letters, letters. Let me ask you this, Dominic. I understand that the circulation for that particular month was only 50,000. Is that true? Was that an additional 50,000? Well, I know the circulation went up to one hundred and eighty five thousand copies per month and admitted the publication about half a million dollars.

[00:07:48.540]

So. Well, I mean, that's that's neither here nor there about the amount of money, I was interested in the circulation. You say that the circulation was about a hundred and eighty five thousand after these stories began to be published, when there is a possibility that they could receive 50,000 letters. Let's let's just say that the circulation was actually a hundred and fifty thousand for round figures, and that would be a third of the readers that sent in a letter.

[00:08:16.860]

Of course, that would be a tremendous amount. I mean, that's very unusual. But let's face it, if we're going to accept that circulation figure, and I have no reason to doubt the word of Ziff-Davis as a publishing outfit, and if they had that amount of circulation, well, they could have received credit for that one particular statement. And it wasn't just Ziff-Davis that made this claim. It was primarily

Illustration by Richard S. Shaver depicting life in the caves as he knew it. Each detail of the picture exists as shown, according to Mr. Shaver. The front cover by another artist, also depicts life in the caves.

Palmer himself that made this claim. Well, now, let me let me ask you this.

[00:08:45.630]

Are you familiar with ABC Audit Bureau of Circulation? That's an unbiased organization that determines the circulation of any publication that is a member of their organization. Now, you can't pay them off. In other words, no money, whatever. In other words, you couldn't even offer them enough money at any time that maybe they would try to give you a break and add a little additional circulation to their report. Now, if Ziff-Davis I'm very sure I don't know about in those days, but Jeff Davis, I'm very sure, is a member of the Audit Bureau of Circulation.

[00:09:33.360]

So any circulation figures that would be given out by the Ziff-Davis publishers or any member of Audit Bureau of Circulation would be an accurate circulation figure. Now, if this figure was given out, that figure of one hundred and eighty five thousand by the Ziff- Davis publishers, then you and I can bet our bottom dollar that that was the legitimate.

[00:10:00.330]

Paid circulation, there is no exaggeration, there's no cream that's been put on top or anything to pump it up. There is a fantastic circulation for the magazine of the paper at the premium. I wouldn't be in a position to judge. I don't know what would be

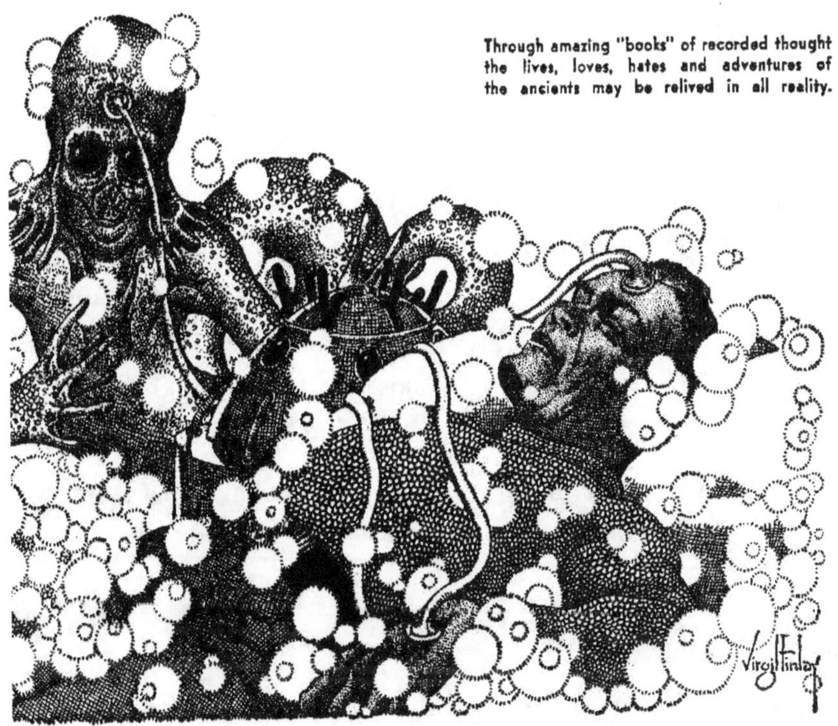

Through amazing "books" of recorded thought
the lives, loves, hates and adventures of
the ancients may be relived in all reality.

considered good circulation for a science fiction publication. I might just say this to you that I understand that *Life* has a circulation of, I think, something like six or seven million. I know that *Faith Magazine* has a circulation of sixty five thousand, and certainly that's that's a a magazine that well, it's directed to a very, very limited group of readers.

[00:10:48.900]

So it's quite possible that they have that. I mean, I think we should at least be fair to Palmer and to Ziff-Davis and to Mr. Shaver, and say that this is quite possible. And if they, if they had one hundred and eighty five thousand readers that month or if they had one hundred eighty five thousand paid circulation, then there is a possibility, as remote as it may seem, that they could receive 50,000 letters. Yeah, well, from what, I hear John, is that there was a paper shortage.

[00:11:23.550]

And as the circulation began to increase and began to get these large figures, they began taking paper from their other magazines in order to keep up the quantity of *Amazing Stories*. In other words, they had, I think, detected publication at the time, and they would borrowed paper so they would publish less of one publication and put out more copies of *Amazing Stories*. That's what I heard John. I mean, I can tell you this. What did you hear this from Palmer or is this known in the trade?

[00:12:00.580]

This is sort of known in the trade. I mean, this is sort of a trade rumor, so to speak. And, I myself know that at the time, I was very interested and extremely interested in Shaver and then in Palmer, of course, because I did like *Amazing Stories,* I like to read as science fiction, and I found that they became extremely fascinating. And, I was there profounding *The Shaver Mystery,* and sort of putting it over its true.

[00:12:28.950]

And I myself used to have trouble sometimes finding a newsstand, which had the magazine about four or five days after it hit. It seemed like during the war, during during the time when the show, the Shaver Mystery was running, or more or less every month during the war. That was during the war. It was just near the end of the war. Actually, it really started in 1945 when he hit with that one terrific story that *I remember Lemuria.*

[00:12:59.670]

And it seemed to keep everybody off. But the people began writing in and saying, is true, this thing happened to me and it's happened to my neighbor. And Shaver is telling the truth. And they began backing him up right up to 100 percent. An interesting thought, at least I think it's rather interesting to think about for a moment. I was always under the impression that the majority nef people who purchased or did purchase at that time *Amazing Stories*, that these were science fiction fans.

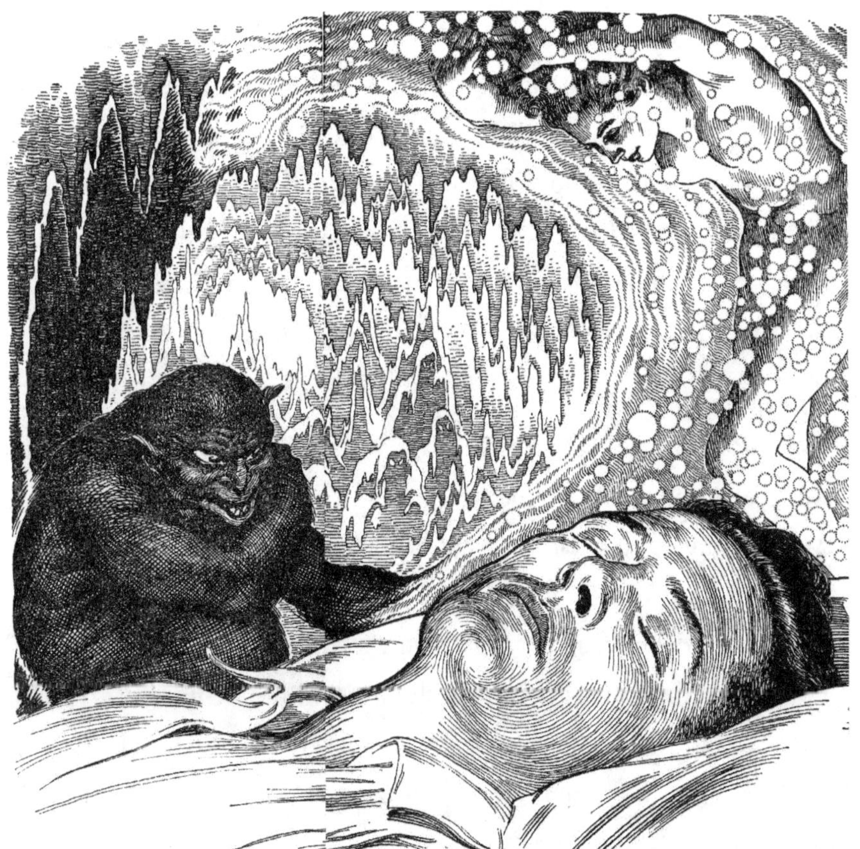

Good and evil—the hideous and the beautiful—battled for his sleeping mind.

[00:13:35.790]

Now, do you think that science fiction fans would be the type who would write in letters and say, I believe this, this happened to me and all because they're so accustomed to these wild, fantastic tales that they've been reading the magazine for any length of time? Oh, John, I don't really know because, I noticed that they're after this story came out, when the word got around or whether it was the cover or whatever it was. But I noticed many of my friends weren't interested in science fiction, began buying *Amazing Stories*.

[00:14:08.190]

And in all probability, some of the science fiction fans. And I can't say percentage wise or to what degree, but I'd say some of the science fiction fans did buy the Shaver story. Besides buying *Amazing Stories*, wasn't it also true that they were sold to Shaver clubs at that time, and many people there want to **Shaver Mystery** Clubs started and they were more or less we could liken them to the social clubs of today. And the strangest thing is, actually is the Shaver in his original stories.

[00:14:43.690]

Explain what people call the source of mystery today. Actually Shaver had it long before the so-called social mystery of it came into the headlines. When is he the one that put some pretty good success stories out? Shaver, Shaver did, and they weren't exactly success stories. He didn't call success stories you? No, he had a

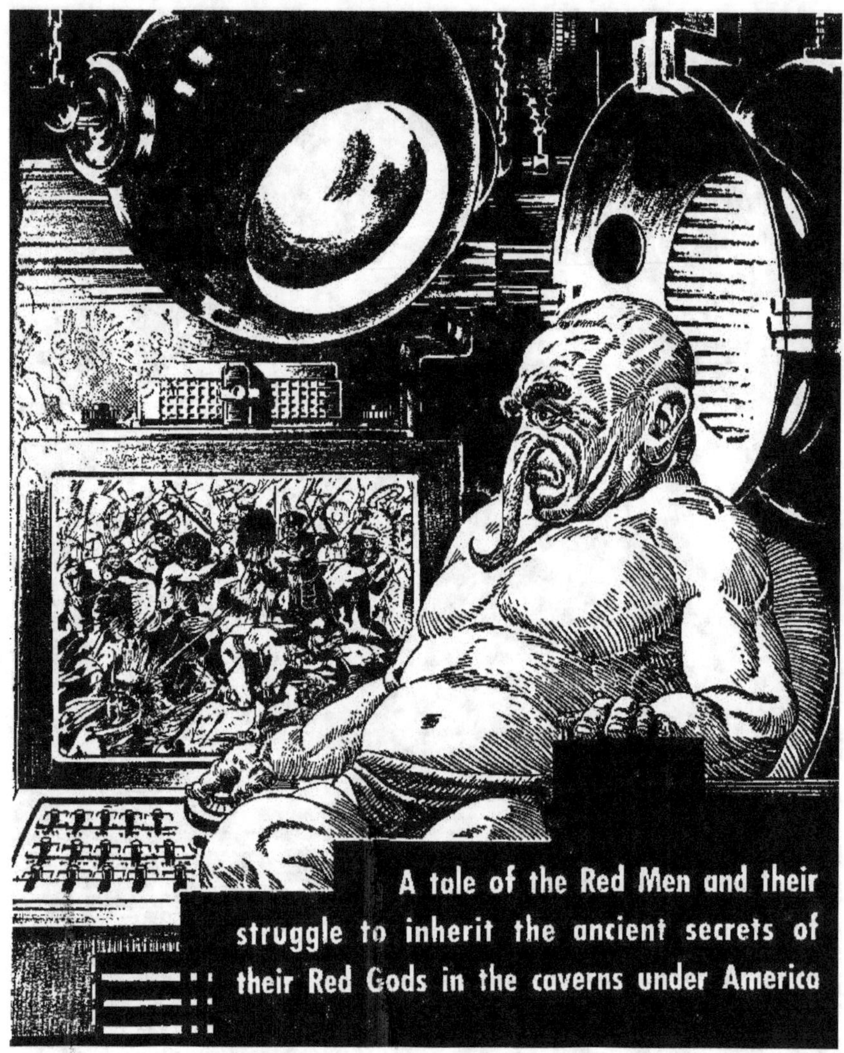
A tale of the Red Men and their struggle to inherit the ancient secrets of their Red Gods in the caverns under America

different name for them and he avoid using a lot of , if you took a notice in his writings. But I don't know whether it was Shaver's touch or whether it was promised touch, but which gave it that sort of ancient Hindu mythological angle sort of.

[00:15:23.460]

And they were terrific stories. They were, I wouldn't say they were the best in science fiction by no means. But it was the the footnotes to the stories which made them interesting, in other words, would probably expand one paragraph of Shaver's into two pages of the script in the magazine. And then below this, he would more or less try and reclaim what was the supposed truths hidden in pomace rendition of Shaver's so-called blot record receptions. I've been listening, and I may have missed the point.

[00:16:03.810]

Did you bring out that I hear this someplace else about the fact that Mr Shaver was receiving these messages through some type of welding equipment? Yes, he was John, going to bring this up. Well, then why do we come in with this thought record? Well, the information that Shaver received on this welding equipment was information which pertained to the history of what we may say of life on the earth itself on this planet. And these records supposedly went back 20000 years into history, the history of the planet, on this planet?.

Harte Manville lowered him-
self into a cavern; and found a mad world.

[00:16:47.790]

And he thought he was getting this record, which was a recording left behind by the race of beings who inhabited the planet before the present era, these beings were known as **Titans**, Shaver claims. And later on, in some of the stories of some of these thought records, they come out as Atlans (A-t-l-a-n-s), which would give us to presuppose that there was sort of an Atlantis theme involved in Shaver's history. Did he ever mention anything about **Atlantis**? Well, he claimed that the continent of Atlantis and **Lemuria** or **Mu**, as it was known, did exist and was part of the ancient inhabited colonies of these **Titans**.

[00:17:39.540]

But one thing Shaver did say, and that was that Atlantis did not necessarily think, in other words, it did not fall beneath the sea as we have come to more or less suppose. But actually the sinking was a misinterpretation. What happened to it? And according to Shaver, while Shaver claim that the Atlantis, or I can't recall exactly which one, now was a long time ago that I read this particular, I thought you were going to claim that you were there at the time.

[00:18:08.310]

Well, I don't know. I might be a reincarnated Dero or Tero. Tero or Dero? Well, I don't know. I guess you could use some sort of a free hand style on it. Who is determined to say that you have your name thrown out there that day? DE, according to white men term from the alphabet from the chart, which are supposedly Shaver received from these thought records of the. Lemuria was so DE, so DE it would be pronounced in the alphabet as D, so in row, D-row, stand in the alphabet with the phonetic alphabet.

[00:18:50.910]

And as Shaver playing this alphabet, each letter in the alphabet was descriptive of a particular mental concept or sequence of mental concepts. It was sort of a basic source alphabet for the human language. What would be DB, D would be disinterment energy and it would be pronounced DE and what ROB would are all be are,R would be horror and O stood for orifice or source, so D-row stands for detrimental horror source, and in other words, detrimental row or detrimental ro-bot. But if we converted into modern English, Shaver claims that this Alphabet.

[00:19:33.590]

That works out in most languages except the romance languages. He claims that it doesn't work out so well in the romance languages, but it does work well. It works in the ancient Teutonic dialects and works well in **Sanskrit**. It works on Hindu, Hindustani. Have you ever made any tests? Yes, I have John. A little later in the program, I would like to conduct a test. With your permission? Which you listening to me. Of course. But all right. Now, when I interrupted you, Dominic, I think that you were telling me the correct pronunciation of the word "DERO".

THE FALL OF LEMURIA

Mr. Shaver's Lemurian Alphabet

A—Animal (used AN for short)
B—Be (to exist—often command)
C—See
D—(also used DE) Disintegrant energy; Detrimental (most important symbol in language)
E—Energy (an all concept, including motion)
F—Fecund (use FE as in female—fecund man)
G—Generate (used GEN)
H—Human (some doubt on this one)
I—Self; Ego (same as our I)
J—(see G) (same as generate)
K—Kinetic (force of motion)
L—Life
M—Man
N—Child; Spore; Seed (as ninny)
O—Orifice (a source concept)
P—Power
Q—Quest (as question)
R—(used as AR) Horror (symbol of dangerous quantity of dis force in the object)
S—(SIS) (an important symbol of the sun)
T—(used as TE) (the most important symbol; origin of the cross symbol) Integration; Force of growth (the intake of T is cause of gravity; the force is T; tic meant science of growth; remains as credit word)
U—You
V—Vital (used as VI) (the stuff Messmer calls animal magnetism; sex appeal)
W—Will
X—Conflict (crossed force lines)
Y—Why
Z—Zero (a quantity of energy of T neutralized by an equal quantity of D)

Some "English" Lemurian Words

ABSENT—Animal be sent (one was sent, therefore is not here)
ADDER—A der (the animal is a der, or deadly)
ARREST—Animal stops to rest (the ar syllable means is dangerously stopped)
BEGET—To cause to exist (command to generate the energy of integrance)
BAD—Be a de (to be a destructive force)
BARD—Bar de (one who allays depressing de force, who overjoys us, decreases depression)
BIG—Be I generate (in the act of generation, as pregnant)
BILK—Be ill kinetic (to run away from ill, to dodge—K for movement)
DARK—Detrimental horrible movement (harrowing things we are apt to see "in the dark")
DECEASE—Stopped by de (disintegrated to the point of ceasing to be—death)
DEVIATE—De vital ate (de has eaten the vital force, implication being the thing goes astray because of destructive force)
DEVIL—De vile (to be vile with de; completely destructive)
DROP—De ro power (disintegrance governs power, thus it becomes less, falls)
LADY—Lay de (allay depression; complimentary term)
MAD—Man a de (one who may de, be apt to destroy)
MEAN—Me animal (animal conscious only of self)
MORBID—More be I de (I don't want to be any more, I want to die)
NEE—Child energy (charm)
NEUTRAL—Ne you te ral (attracted by the charm of both parties)
OBSCENE — Orifice see charm (orifice meant source of life, thus the meaning is evident)
PACT—Power act (an empowered act)
PEAL—Power all (power and all combine to give a loud sound)
PRISON—Price on (to hold for ransom)
QUIT—Quest you I te (get someone else to do good)
VAN—Vital animal (the leader)
ZEAL—Zero all (foolish ardor—to zeal)

THE END

[00:20:15.820]

Oh, that's right. But we have to remember that there isn't only Dero. It is also also Tero supposedly living in these caverns. And there's another thing we have to consider, when we say caverns beneath the earth, they don't necessarily have to be below sea level, actually, because, as Shaver explained, many of the mountain ranges which are above sea level, contains the vast caverns which run for thousands of miles beneath the earth. And we, of course, do realize that there are many unexplored areas of the earth which consist of thousands and thousands of square miles.

[00:20:57.480]

I, I'd even go as far as to say there's also some part of the globe which hasn't even been flown over. And, I think you should know something about that. What do you think about the amount of unexplored areas under the surface? There are many, many places, I believe, down that have never been explored before. In fact, even in our United States here, of course the Tibet, and all those places have not been explored. Yeah, Amalia it is a very

[00:21:24.300]

unknown territory. I was just wondering Dominic, if you could tell our listeners, because there is the possibility that some of them didn't hear the discussion, the time that we had Jeff Robinson, is that it? Jack was here that evening. Can you to give us a little recap on that, what happened to him? Well, John, I wouldn't try to atemp to emulate Jack, because Jack actually loved the story. He was part of it. And I'll do my best to recall it.

[00:21:55.740]

Of course, I would never be able to tell it quite as convincingly as Jack does, because he is the man that happen to, he is the man that knew this person. I can't recall that person's name now, if you'll recall it?. I don't remember, John. Jack was living in a furnished room at the time, I believe. And there was this artists, who Jack became acquainted with. And Jack claimed that this fellow had a strange hobby, if I recall correctly, of creating jewelry out of buttons, Juleanna Buttons, he did the collecting buttons and then he used to put little things on them and put them and created this sort of a custom jewelry.

[00:22:42.720]

And Jack got to know him very well. He got in the men's confidence, and this man cleaned or he told Jack this in a more or less of period of time, Jack was able to derive from the man the fact that this man at one time or another had been on a prospecting trip into the desert country in California. And this man, claimed that he was kidnapped by the Dero and that he had been kept in the caverns for, I forget how many years old, he was two years, he argued.

[00:23:25.290]

And that in some way I can't remember the exact detail. But the man found himself wandering in New York City. There wasn't.

Because there some story about that he was missing, you had something? Yes, he had a eight hundred dollars in his pocket and two years later, he found himself walking on Times Square. I believe there was a guy found the same eight hundred dollars and it seemed that no time had lapsed. And yet he discovered that it was two years later that two years out of his life seemed to disappeared.

[00:23:59.940]

He had no knowledge of it. That was the idea of a job and plus the fact that the man was an artist, if I remember. And the man used to paint these very weird landscapes, which looked like landscapes from another world. They consisted of odd, odd color combinations in, in color and harmonious tones. The paintings, he said, had a great depth to them. And they had this very weird quality. No matter who would look at them, they could sort of sense something alien about them, about the scenes depicted in these pictures.

[00:24:36.600]

And the man, Jack, said the man was extremely clean. He was a nice person. He was very went out of his way to be kind to everyone. And he was a vegetarian. He would not eat meat. What was the reason this? It might have been and might have been that the Deros, he probably had seen things that I wouldn't want to discuss. I mean, he probably had seen some pretty horrible things in the caverns.

[00:25:03.330]

And I doubt very much if he had a full recall of what happened. But, Jack said, he remembers going down into the caverns, being kidnapped and taken into the caverns, and then there was some type of mechanism attached to his head. And Jack said this man still had the scars on his temples where these mechanisms supposedly still don't have the scars, where these mechanisms was attached to his temples. What was the reason for these mechanism to be able to work?

[00:25:34.770]

The way I see it John, I'm looking at it from the viewpoint of what we know. I'd say that these mechanisms probably made him into a slave or a robot. What he claims that he has no knowledge at all. He, he believes that, that is what happened to him. Did Shaver ever, ever say anything about the possibility of people being made slaves? Definitely John, this was one of his main points. Another idea, and definitely that was one of his main points. He brought up missing persons and he claimed that the Deros, for thousands of years, were kidnapping people from the surface and doing it in such a underhanded way that it just nobody ever just thought of it.

[00:26:15.000]

I mean, this is a fantastic amount of persons missing every year. And it's certainly possible to say that they have to be taken somewhere. It's difficult to deal with the bureau, as we have in the United States here, to just disappear. I mean, why Social Security numbers? Why is it so difficult to disappear? Well, because ID is more or less required when you apply for a job, if you apply for a defence job in particular, if you apply for a job in a plant which is subsidised by the government, what would happen if you.

[00:26:49.980]

Dominic, I don't know what the rules may be. And I just don't I mean, now that you've made that statement, what would happen if you left your home in New Jersey and went to another part of this country and assumed another name? And you made application for a Social Security card? Would they question you and refuse to give you one? I said, to be honest with you, John, it's so long ago since I applied for my Social Security card.

[00:27:18.780]

I mean, because you applied for one many years ago. I mean, let us assume that you go to another part of the country, and you take on a new name. You change your name, not legally. In other words, you don't go to court or anything like that, and you change your name to Augi Roberts. Could you walk into a Social Security office and apply for a new card, or would they ask you what happened to your old card?

[00:27:48.670]

Oh John, I think that I could do, I could actually, I agree with you. I think, I could get a new card. Right, I think so. You could get a new Social Security card. What is the big problem about getting

ID? Well, age would becoming a major factor, major? I think what would have to do it? Well, I doubt if anybody would be foolish enough to falsify any papers where they would have to apply to a draft board or when they would have to apply to any job which required some type of civil service.

[00:28:17.790]

You don't have to take that type of job. In other words, if you're trying to get away from somebody or some situation in the community that you now reside in, and you go to another community in another part of the country. In other words, I'm interested in the statement you made about missing. Now, if you go to another part of the country, and you get a new draft card, it's quite true, you probably will not get a job with the FBI, but you could get a job working in a restaurant.

[00:28:48.250]

You could possibly get a job working in a gasoline station as an attendant. And what would be the reason that you need an ? I agree wholeheartedly with that contention, John. I'm not sure that isn't the point that interests me. It's not just missing persons. According to what I could discover, the FBI has listed about a hundred and twenty thousand people per year in the United States missing, which is quite a lot of people. And I'm not interested in the majority of missing persons.

[00:29:21.550]

What I am interested in is the minority groups which disappear without apparent cause or reason. In other words, the fellow whose wife tells them or tells his wife he leaves is cold. He leaves everything, he practically owns and runs down to the corner drugstore, and never comes back again. And then it just so happens that there's a lot of there's a lot of reasons for these things to happen. But certainly, I can't give you the answer. The reason for every person who has ever disappeared, because I don't know the people, but there's a possibility that a man just reaches a point in life that he's going to pass it in.

[00:30:03.990]

He wants to just divorce himself from all past associations. He doesn't pack a bag. He doesn't take a toothbrush, a razor blade. He doesn't even go to the bank, and take all the money up. He's got nineteen dollars and eighty four cents in his pocket, and he leaves. Sure. It's a tragic thing. It's a tragic situation for his family. But why wouldn't it be possible to do this? And let me ask you another question. Is it illegal to leave for providing that you don't take the car that you own with you?

[00:30:39.120]

Oh, no. I think that, I think it is. After all, if the man is very ill, he can be charged with desertion. That's right. Let's forget about marriage. Remember, the man is not married. Let's assume that I'm a married man who who had been working for some company, the

X, Y, Z Corporation, possibly as their sales manager is not married. His parents passed away a number of years ago, and he may be sitting in the local pub and he thinks to himself, why?

[00:31:12.350]

What is the big struggle for? And he calls the bartender over and he says, Charlie, what do I owe you? Charlie figured it out. You owe me three dollars and twenty cents. So, he throws in four single dollars bill, and waits a navy cent tip. He takes up and walks out. Never goes back to his apartment. Doesn't pick up the attaché case, doesn't take any of the books, anything, just disappear. Well, what we've done John you where we got it down to two categories anywhere we got those who have good reason for disappearing.

[00:31:47.970]

And now we have a percentage of the hundred and twenty thousand, who have no apparently good reason for disappearing, but who disappear on the spur of the moment. And what would you consider the statistical part of that type that you're discussing now? Just walk up? Yeah, I don't think, I can give you an answer to that question any more, than you can give me an answer any more, and tell me what percentage you think of the people that have been grabbed. Well, I don't know what have you by the Delo.

[00:32:19.470]

I don't particularly think anything in particular on that particular point. But what I do say is that the possibility exists. And the fact is one hundred and twenty thousand people is a lot of people, some say out of a hundred and twenty thousand people, at least maybe five or 10 or maybe even a little more. Well, remember John, we're only talking of one country now. This concerns the whole earth. It's not only one country. Well, suppose they were picked up by the police for some reason or other minor infractions or they did something like that and their fingerprints were checked.

[00:32:56.520]

Wouldn't anything bring out their original name? That happens every day of the year. Mean that happens every day by why would a fingerprint that my fingerprints are not registered anyplace? To my knowledge, to my knowledge no, I know from the army service and so on. That's right. But no, those records are not kept. The FBI keeps the Army records? I know if I do anything wrong that I might. I don't know. I don't know about that.

[00:33:25.560]

Actually, what I was getting at there is that there are countries in the world who don't keep us close to check on missing persons as in the United States or they haven't got the law enforcement agencies we have here. And they can. India, for instance, there could be thousands upon thousands of people were missing in India and very few people would know about it because of the every year the lack of police citizenry working to stop or alleviate the condition of people just disappearing.

[00:34:01.620]

In India, you have people who are actually dying of starvation while they're on their feet practically. And actually, I doubt if statistics are kept to any great accuracy in India. So, we'll take just India alone, a country like India. Why go to India all of a sudden this happened here in United Sates, and all over, 120,000 people. Dominic, I don't know why we should think on India. We got one hundred and twenty thousand people missing. And you have implied that there is a possibility that maybe there's a percentage, maybe only 10 people out of a hundred and twenty thousand people that are kidnapped by the Deros?

[00:34:39.600]

Well, we first we have to sort of break it down into categories, and then we have to figure from the dew point of percentage. How can you break anything down into categories when you know nothing about? I don't mean to. And I think that by going to a missing persons bureau or speaking to a missing persons expert, we can get a statistical average of why people disappear. And by breaking down known average we could arrive, and deduce those that according to the probability ratio, would not disappear by any normal explanation.

[00:35:18.280]

Do most people disappear in remote areas of the United Sates? Well, I would put it this way. I don't know. Disappeared from from, say, small communities or people walking in the country somewhere. I would say this that a person living in a small community, if he disappears, it would be more noticeable. But it would also be it would also be less known to those who live in larger communities. Along the Deros usually operate in remote parts of the country.

[00:35:48.570]

Well, you know, strangely enough, that isn't so. In fact, according to Shaver, many of the larger cities in the United States have a surface zero population. Is it possible to disappear right in your own room? Well, there's another fantastic claim by Richard S. Shaver, and he claims that the Deros have in their possession a mechanisms which can buy scientific knowledge or means by utilizing certain ways create what we may term a state of teleport in the human body. In other words, people could disappear from a closed and locked room.

[00:36:34.770]

Are you familiar with the story? I'm sure you are down with the kept I have of this fellow who sent it to us and he made the claim that while he was laying in bed one night, he remembered the story we told or was told a number of months ago with **Harlan Ellison**, that he was to make a large noise and start yelling, I want to see a Dero, that the jurors would come to him. At this point, I want to bring in more you strangely enough, I'm going to have to disagree with that.

[00:36:59.920]

I don't think that any particular fit like when you add a more or less perform would bring a Dero to, to teleport you to the caverns. Well no, this fellow made the claim that, I think promenade that claim, actually, I think promenade that claim in a letter that he wrote to Gerard, in a letter that he wrote to me?, in reference to **Harlan Ellison,** in which he said that if Ellison would take your shoes off and throw it on the yelled the top of his voice.

[00:37:38.830]

Well, personally, I think if fellow did something like that, I think that the Deros wouldn't take them away. I think it would be a minimun in the white coats. I what, I wanted to say was that this fellow here made a loud noise, and he wanted to see a Dero, and he was laying down in bed. Maybe, he went to sleep, I don't know. But he said he felt something, grabbed his leg and start checking all the bed that, you know, you want to tell him.

[00:38:03.550]

You made a statement there that I don't particularly buy, but I don't think, I've never actually seen a Dero, which I could prove was a Dero. I've seen people who could fit the description, probably both physiologically and mentally, both. But I certainly never seen anyone, I could prove was a Dero. I don't know, . I can say that the Dero would not come to your room where you could perform that. That's strange. Know if I'm in trouble.

[00:38:33.310]

I think actually that **Ray Palmer** was trying to be facetious and at the same time, he was trying to make a point. In other words, actually, acording to that letter, and I haven't got it, I have it someplace in in my files out in Parsippany, New Jersey, my home. But I know that he, he was pretty peeved to **Harlan Ellis** because Harland had made a couple of statements ridiculing Ray on the program. He ridiculed Ray Palmer. And I think this is the reason that Ray wrote that letter.

[00:39:14.200]

There was something, some discussion on the program. Holland made a statement that he met **Ray Palmer** in an elevator and they were going up or coming down from one of the floors in the hotel at a science fiction convention. And the two of them were in the elevator alone. Plus, naturally, the operator and **Colin** made the statement that Ray Palmer said that the whole thing was a farce, that he had written it to increase the circulation in *Amazing Stories*.

[00:39:50.100]

Well, of course, this is fine, this is something that he should do. He should try to increase the circulation of any publication that he may be the editor of. But to do it in that way would be wrong. Now, whether Ray ever said this or not, I will never be in a position to say. But **Ray Palmer** has denied it emphatically. He claims that he never spoke to **Harland Allison**. I shouldn't say that he never spoke to Harland, but he never discussed the Shaver Mystery.

[00:40:18.990]

You know funny thing Dominick, if anything, you told me that the correct pronunciation is Deros in the last 20 minutes, you've been saying no, what is it? I guess it's force of habit, John. A lot of people say Dero. And that's what I thought is a lazy way of doing it. Actually, a lazy way of doing it, a lazy way of doing it. All right. I think we at the time that I am directed to take care of a little business Dominick, I think that I'm sorry.

[00:40:50.120]

Don't you know, I've read them many times over the years, John, as Oggie Robertson, Dominic Lucchesi. Hi, hi. And, I am into a discussion. We were talking about the possibility of a small percentage. In fact, you didn't even say small percentage. I'm assuming that this is what you think anyway, that a percentage of the hundred and twenty thousand missing people that statistics tell us are missing every year. Some small percentage may have been kidnapped by the Deros. A percentage of the hundred and twenty thousand missing people that statistics tell us are missing every year, some small percentage, ...

[00:41:40.130]

may have been kidnapped by the Deros, yes John or no incidents. And I like the way you started. "Yes. John". In other words.

Actually you really believe this? Believe that a certain percentage of missing persons cannot be accounted for by normal explanation? Oh no please, I agree with you, that they cannot be accountable any person who is missing and they've never been able to trace them. Then they cannot account for. Know what my condition is during the certain ones. Certain of these missing people cannot be accounted for by any normal explanation.

[00:42:24.230]

What I know by that is by any known cause if. I leave my home. And they never find the body, they never get a letter on me. They know nothing about me, they never hear me. Would you call that by normal means? You would become a statistic here. That's right. So you, Dominique Lucchesi, may take this statistic and say that the Deros kidnapped. There's a possibility, John. I don't know, they might kidnap your wife. That is the thing you honestly believe this.

[00:43:05.850]

Do I honestly believe this, that the Deros particularly kidnap anyone ? I don't know, actually. And we were waiting for them here in order for you to try and clarify this one particular point. A hundred and twenty thousand people disappeared, and we were discussing the fact that many of these people disappeared for good reason. Then, there's others who do not appear to disappear for any good reason. In other words, they just go down to the corner store for a pack of cigarettes and then never come back.

[00:43:42.240]

And John had arrived at that one particular point there where he said there is also a possibility, that these people decided on the spur of the moment to disappear at that particular time for no reason. Now, we granted this this we have two types of people that disappeared. We have the people who disappeared for good cause because whether they're evading norms or whether they just want to give it all up and just disappear. And we have the people who disappeared who have no apparent foreknowledge of this disappearance.

[00:44:18.120]

Another way, they don't think about this fact that it is predetermined. They just happen to do it at spur of the moment. And in order for a disappearance to be successful, it would have to appear that way, wouldn't it? I mean, the very fact that someone is missing and cannot be traced seems to me to be abnormal. And the very fact that someone wants not to be traced means, that he would plan it as if it were the most casual thing is worthwhile does.

[00:44:41.700]

Not necessarily, because actually, I think I myself, if I was going to disappear, I would make sure that I would have certain things with me. I certainly wouldn't disappear in shirtsleeves, would disappear in my undershirt in the summertime or disappear in my slippers, so to speak. If I wanted a successful disappearance. I mean, I don't know how I know. The most famous case is **Judge Crater** for I know a little bit about because I know some of the people in the bar association.

[00:45:13.480]

The very thing, we're going to have an exposé of the **Judge Crater** case this morning. No, I know, I know how what led up to it? I mean, the rest he just walked out of the bar association one night. He was going to meet his wife for dinner. He said goodnight to the elevator operator. He got into a cab, and he was never seen again. Now, I think this, I don't, I don't know why or how **Judge Crater** disappeared.

[00:45:38.140]

Well, I assure you that, if I wanted to make a successful disappearance, I wouldn't go to the bank and draw out a lot of money, and I wouldn't send the order. No luggage, and I wouldn't have my have deposits transferred to other banks, and other items that I had a tremendous cash account. I would walk out if it was, and I would say I'm going to walk out with a t shirt on, and just disappear. This is because everybody said what could have happened to him. He didn't take any money, he didn't steal any money.

[00:46:15.270]

He didn't leave the bank. You know what I mean is still the tale. He didn't take any luggage. He didn't even take his favorite electric razor or his favorite pipe that he smoked. Yeah. Then this happens all leads up to the fact that the most important point to making a successful disappearance is to make it look like it isn't a disappearance. I was wondering, John, If Miller Judge Crater does create a little bit of an elevator, and I don't know, maybe he got into a taxi cab and disappeared.

[00:46:43.890]

Or the only thing is that, I mean, there are rumors. I still want to stand at the Bar Association library. I mean, the last time he's ever been found. I don't know, man. I know, I'm not an expert on disappearances. Actually, what I am doing here is we were describing this mystery, which was started by Richard S Shaver. In *Amazing Stories* that was back in nineteen forty five. Now, I know about one of is more or less contentions was that many of the people who disappeared, and he didn't give any particular percentage.

[00:47:22.080]

He said many of the people who disappeared are kidnapped by these Deros who reside in the caverns beneth the earth. One of the Deros won't... According to Shaver they use them as slaves and for their own nefarious purposes, the Deros are supposedly a degenerate race of beings very cruel, very evil, very negative. And it was Shaver's contention that they did not stop or would not stop at kidnapping the surface beings, taking them to the caverns for experimental purposes, for purposes of utilizing them for work and for various other purposes, which I would not care to mention.

[00:48:12.660]

All the percentage, 160,000 successful disappearances that no one knows anything about and say roughly, say a few percent of these were caused by Deros own very probable that a small percentage, say two or three or five people would have escaped from the Deros, and would have come come back and tell, we have definite or not definite, but we have stories about people who have escaped from the Deros. We always have. Gray Barker visited a woman in Pennsylvania.

[00:48:47.780]

I believe it. I think we should tell our listeners about Gray Barker, there is the possibility that some may be listening, and needed to hear about that particular night. Oh, I see that. Gray Barker is a researcher. He is a successful businessman who went into social research. He got extremely interested, due to a case of the Cold War, the West Virginia monster, where these people in Virginia cited some form of things. And later on, Gray became associated with Mr. Roberts and myself through the International Flying Saucer Bureau, which was run by a person by the name of Albert Kay Bender, and one evening, three men went to Bender's house, wearing dark suits and homburg hats, and Mister Bender was no longer talking.

[00:49:47.480]

Strangely enough, there are parts of the Shaver Mystery which seem to parallel the Bender Mystery. But getting back to Mr. Barker. Mr. Barker visited this woman in Pennsylvania. I can't recall the woman's name. It is on record. I have it Oggie probably has somewhere at home. And this woman claimed that she had actually lived in the caverns for many years, and her story more or less. And though, she didn't have any amazing stories in her house at the time or she didn't read science fiction, she happened to be a very old woman at the time when Gray visited her, she did claim that she had lived in the caverns, and her story paralleled what Shaver claimed to be fact.

[00:50:43.220]

Now, I happened to start something new, which was interesting, and I'd like to bring it up at this time. When I said that this is a Bender incident, the Bridgeport Incident. And there is Bender being picked up by three men. Strangely enough, Ray Palmer informed a number of people that the FBI investigated Shaver. And informs in his own words, what they told him was one fact that's quite from, from one fact which made it difficult to drop the mystery.

[00:51:25.270]

In other words, what these FBI men told Richard S. Shaver made it difficult for Shaver to drop the mystery, not that he would have anyway. I doubt that. But what was this thing, what they told him?

I have never been able to find out. And it's just as much a mystery as what the three men who visited Mr. Albert K. Benders told him, which frightened him, and frightened him so badly, that he didn't eat nor sleep for two days.

[00:51:53.980]

Was it already three days? For three days? And prior to that, both Augie, and myself had known Mr. Bender very intimately. We were very good friends of Benders who were helping him put out this magazine that he used to publish. He had a worldwide organization, three days before the event occurred. He had received an article from me, which dealt with some form of interplanetary power, if I recalled correctly, it was for a new column, which was to go into his little publication which was called *Space Review*.

[00:52:33.250]

And three days prior to Bender's visit, Bender had accepted this article, and told me the that *Space Review* would be published as usual, and that there would be some startling things contained there. And unfortunately, that particular issue was faced with a review which Bender referred to. It was never published. It just never got to the printing, I don't think so. Did he did it? One final issue was that Bender had to revise it at the at the request of the three men..

[00:53:12.220]

There are lots of sorts of publications, lots of people interested in social research. For instance, Jim Mosley, who's a very fine researcher, which is a very fine. So it's a man who's never been silenced since Van Tassel. So that's why we have violence. One single claim, all sorts of contacts, is how it manager who's never been visited by three men in black. So there's one thing, though, and around that time it was the beginning of the sort of groups and they silenced the top group at that time.

[00:53:44.230]

And as why wouldn't they continue this policy if they found out they made an error? I wasn't, wasn't Gray Barker by this contention that he's not the only one who's been fired. Several people with that. These three men of evidence. There was, there was a general of the Australian Flying Saucer Bureau. There was a fellow up in New Zealand, a fellow up in Canada. All of these have been silenced and frightened. Yeah, well, this, this point about get this straight, Ray Palmer said that there was one point that the FBI made mentioned to him, not to Palmer, to Shaver, to Shaver that would not permit Shaver to drop it, because it was so startling, while he was away, and then never went on to say what the statement was that I mean, forgive me for sounding a little harsh, but this sounds like a typical Palmer action.

[00:54:37.570]

I mean, I recall a certain piece of metal that was lost somewhere outside Seattle that was supposedly definite proof of a saucer landing at Murray Island incident. Would you please tell me why you think that is typical Palmer action? Actually, just what I mentioned or what what is one particular incident that you mentioned? You know, typical Palmer actions. In other words, Palmer claims in some book to have lost a piece of metal. Is that a typical Palmer claims to have a piece of metal?

[00:55:08.410]

What was that? A typical claims?, then, the FBI took away from him. And then it was lost in an airplane crash, on a airplane crash is on record. Two men lost their lives in the crash. I don't think Palmer would more or less. How would you say it expressed slightly anything such as a crash where two men lost their lives. Augie Roberts is one of the few people, I know who actually went to Murray Island and investigated the scene of this incident.

[00:55:41.470]

And I think that you do find that certain points in the story didn't check as far as you were able to ascertain. Just one good point that I would like to know, and would like to get the answers of. And that was the fact that why did the Coast Guard in a three sets of Coast Guardsmen there, and they operate this lighthouse? Actually, Murray island is a lighthouse station. Why three days later, they were taken off this Light House and sent to another part of the country and three were sent in.

[00:56:13.660]

They regularly rotate these dependants at light houses right after this incident?. Well, with more on that, the incident could have an answer. It could have happened on such, a such a day and the next next day was the regular day to be relieved. We have to allow that possibility. That is true. And in other words Ben, what you're trying to say is that you do not believe in the science group, is that correct? No. What I'm trying to say is that I don't like anybody coming out and saying that.

[00:56:42.310]

Unfortunately, no. Let me put it again. I don't like anyone coming out and saying something that there was one fact revealed which made it impossible to drop this mystery. Unfortunately, I don't know or cannot reveal this fact. This to me is a journalistic stunt. Well, Ben actually, let's put it this way. In other words, there is something called act, which if you, if you knew about what shake you to the very roots, but unfortunately, I can't tell you about it, doesn't that possibility exists?

[00:57:12.130]

I think there are many men in this world right at this very moment in a position where they know things that would be very shaky in context, and they cannot tell due to security reasons. No, I don't see where your point goes. So much for this strikingly parallels this incident, the Maury incidents where there was a there was a piece of metal that was supposed to be definitive proof about the interplanetary origin of flying saucers, because, first of all, the metal defied chemical analysis of something else.

[00:57:45.250]

And the same thing was being rushed and all of a sudden it disappeared. And this, again, is the fact that isn't there. I mean, this thing that happened, it's happened twice so far with Palmer's connection with saucers, as I'm just pointing out, that this is a method which, I am very suspicious of as far as I don't, I don't like it. It's sort of untidy as far as I'm concerned, referring to the fact that unfortunately cannot be exhibited.

[00:58:14.470]

This is like taking a secret file into a courtroom, and pointing to it, and saying, within the secret file documents that prove that this man is the worst kind of monster. Unfortunately, we cannot open the file, but we should convict this man. I mean, it is it is it is it a lot of trick, actually? Well, tell me Ben, what's assume the hypotheses that you, and I were investigating a certain phenomena in reference to flying saucers, and you happened to obtain a metallic object or a space quark or a space instrument of some type that would definitely establish the fact that this particular vehicle is manufactured by a superior technology far beyond our own.

[00:59:03.670]

And the FBI came to your house, and they said to you, Ben, we don't want you to divulge the information about this particular clock. In other words, we don't want to say anything, said anything else you want. But don't mention this space clock, this speed instrument. Don't mention you as a good citizen. We're putting you on, your honor, not to state this one particular fact of the incident. State anything else you want. Say you the saucer, say you were there, but don't state this particular fact.

[00:59:42.250]

And then you, as my co-worker, in attempting to arrive at a solution to this problem. Correct me, what I would not you would not say to me, well, Don , you're wasting your time. You might stop right now. I happen to know what the answer is, but I can't tell you. Stop wasting your money. Don't take any more photographs. And it's useless, because I know, you mean to tell me you wouldn't tell me anything at all.

[01:00:08.890]

I tell you exactly what I would do. Unfortunately, it's a hypothetical case, so it can never be proven. And it may sound a little bit of a shame, but I for one, am certain the FBI would never approach me in that respect. And if they did, I would tell them to go jump in the lake. Well, I don't think you'd get away with it. I don't think you would. That I tell them to declare that declare this object....

[01:00:31.390]

national security materials are classified in a way that we would immediately or they didn't take this away from Ray Palmer. They made him promise that this does not sound, like I'm familiar with FBI technique, but that does not sound like FBI technique. You don't get promises from people. If something is important to the national security, it is not in your possession anymore. It is classified taken away. In other words, what you're saying is that a man must be about forty two years old, I believe.

[01:01:01.870]

Is that right? I believe so. That a man has lived 42 years, is not entitled to two particular incidents in his life, which don't make sense to Ben Isquith, as far as flying saucers are concerned. And, I feel this way that don't seem to ring true to me. I don't think you actually mean what you said. And, I feel this way, that if you tune in to the FBI ruling, we would miss you around here. Fine, then they have to come into a court.

[01:01:26.740]

And I have to say, I don't think you would get that far to a court like you. People would be missing to do anything that they don't agree with, that if they just taken them without a without a warrant for his arrest or a search warrant for his home or anything like that, they just pick them up, say there is a possibility because I think I hope all good FBI men are sound asleep. And, I certainly need, absolutely surprised. And that is an incredible thing, Augie.

[01:01:59.420]

Well, I certainly hope they would John, actually, because if you're endangering the national security. I think any method would be appropriate at that particular moment. But I rather go by the laws of the books. That's the way I want, I mean, very fortunately, there's still something this country called due process. And the FBI could not lock me up when I assure you that I don't know very much about the law, but I assure you, I have a habeas corpus action search in 24 hours and they'd have to bring me to trial.

[01:02:30.700]

And I have to tell me why I am being brought to trial. And if I go to prison, why I am going to prison. And then, if I'm on stealing the classified security material or something like that, then it would come out. I think there's a much better way. Well, Ben, Do you think that you should have the right to tell them? Right, Yes, I think that, I think they think it's something definitely proves interplanetary origin saucers that people should be told only Augi Roberts and Dominique Lucchesi and Ben is with.

[01:03:02.520]

Know, we were talking about the fact that about. What direct proof of the interplanetary origin of saucers would mean. me now, I have the reason, I'm pretty sure I would behave this way. And the reason why I think this is a very important point is essentially this, is that I think that if it is true that saucers are interplanetary origin, this is the greatest news fact in the last 2000 years, practically. The fact that there is another civilization existing on another planet somewhere that is capable of such a technology that someone, someway made some sort of discovery of our world.

[01:03:43.690]

It's very important from a number of things. I remember one night after the show having coffee with Charlie Lederman talking about it, and more or less, we came to the idea that if this civilization had advanced technology, which could send saucers to our world that far ahead of us in many respects, and history teaches the one sad fact that every time one culture that it's techno technologically superior to another comes in contact with an inferior culture that is inferior because it soon vanished.

[01:04:15.880]

Now, if only for this reason, it's very important about the truth or the forcements of sorts of stories. And it's a report for this reason. I'm very interested in it and for a lot of reasons. I don't like a lot of the wildness, and a lot of the lunatic fringe that go, go on about saucers. Now, there is one concrete fact that I keep on going over which, I will put forth is what I consider to be a fact.

[01:04:43.750]

The one most significant thing in saucers is the one that made me change my mind, the one that made me think there is something flying around up there, which is as far as I could go, was the Washington the **2nd Washington sighting**. That the District of

Columbia right now. This is something that was concrete, was seen by several people, was radar contact and visual contact. At the same time, contact by pursue planes, intercept the ship sent up by the airport.

[01:05:17.680]

This to me, is a concrete fact, not a piece of metal that disappears. And lots of the information told to somebody, which I can't reveal to you, unfortunately, but I stun you, if I told you. This is why I have come a little pedantic on this point. You don't. What I'd like to get out is one point that I'd like to know how we got on flying saucers. When I came in, we were talking about flying saucers, not just mentioned that at one time, but actually we haven't discussed yet, especially from outer space.

[01:05:52.120]

I don't believe in outer space. I'm not talking about saucers from outer space. I'm talking about beings who reside in the caverns beneath the earth. You think that these three men in dark suits were not FBI agents, they were Deros. I don't know Ben, I think personally of my own personal opinion that they were definitely from some agency of the government, our government, our government. And I go so far as to say that, I think that there are agencies in our government which are far more secret and far more powerful than the FBI.

[01:06:27.460]

That's only my opinion on my part, of course. And actually, when we were getting there was the point, and where I was just explaining what Shaver told **Palmer**, and which **Palmer** related as having been told in by Shaver. I certainly did get no definite opinion on what I thought in particular about anything that Shaver had said to Palmer be true or about promising anything to to Shaver or to anyone else. But, what I am doing is recounting the **Shaver Mystery**, which I found extremely interesting, and did not say anything about truth.

[01:07:05.560]

I did not say anything about fact or fiction. That is what, I am trying to find out. I said there are many interesting facets of this particular mystery which are intriguing by their very nature, and which lead one into certain fields of research, which in themselves are extremely interesting. Now, what I would like to do is sort of give a resume to bring you up to date Ben, on the whole mystery, which I haven't done all evening. Actually, from the very beginning.

[01:07:36.100]

I won't go into the actual publication of it. I related that before. What I would like to do is give you Shaver's version of history on Earth. A history, which started, according to Shaver, 20,000 years ago. Shaver claimed that twenty thousand years ago it was a race of beings who lived on the earth and they called themselves Titans and Atlans, which is sort of parallel with with with **Atlantis**. Now, actually, strangely enough now one of the first things I did when I began to read Shaver, I don't believe what I read, contrary to what you may think, there was a book written many years ago.

[01:08:23.860]

I've never had the opportunity of seeing the book, I have only seen it in bibliographies. I've seen it referred to. And that was, I believe and correct me if you know anything about this author, a fellow by the name of, I think it was pronounced **Edward Bulwer**.

Bulwer lightened by an author by the name of r y y y l w way or something like that, NYP or something like that. Now this is something that I saw referred to and he wrote a book called *The Coming Race,* which still referred to an underground race of beings

.

[01:09:03.260]

And he certainly referred to it long before Shaver ever considered receiving voices from a welding machine. Now, Shaver claim that these thought records, which he received with this welding machine, consisted of a history of this planet. Planet Earth is Shaver's claim that these beings actually colonized the Earth all ages ago, way, way back in the past, and that when we get to the twenty thousand year period of the present, I mean, it's strange because twenty thousand years the present.

[01:09:43.280]

But according to Shaver, 20,000 years ago, these people had a superior science. They had vehicles which were similar in design to what we termed today flying saucers. And remember, Shaver was speaking of saucers many, many years, but previous to **Kenneth Arnold's** original scientist. He claimed these Titans and **Atlans** found out that a sun, a star such as ours and its ages, it throws out detrimental rays of energy which cause age according to Shaver. These beings, these **Titans**.

[01:10:23.990]

And they used to live to be 1000 years old. And they found that as the sun age, and the reactions changed, the sun began throwing out these detrimental rays of energy which caused aging. Therefore, they constructed this vast network of caverns beneath the Earth in order to escape the direct rays of the sun, and put enough earth between them as sort of an insulation against this detrimental energy which was radiating from the sun. Now, when they went down to the caverns, they brought with them a vast array of scientific mechanisms, consisting of fantastic machines which could teleport objects, which could move things at a distance, which could melt earth.

[01:11:21.230]

And any known element, actually, they may have had the power of the element, which **Blavatsky** refers to in a book and she called the **Vril, V-r-i-l.** This **Vril** was supposed to be some type of sidereal force, which would mean some type of cosmic energy which they had harnessed, and utilized for their own purposes. Shaver also, claimed that these **Titans** were very large in size. I wouldn't say when he called them giants, I, I wouldn't say that he meant 100 foot tall, but he claimed these people to be about 15, 25 feet tall.

[01:12:02.780]

Now, they went into the caverns, and then, they brough these mechanisms with them, the rays of the sun, which they were no longer exposed to. Now, as these mechanisms in some way drew their energy from the surface. These mechanisms, actually instead of throwing out the beneficial rays they were designed for, after a period of time, these mechanisms became contaminated by a detrimental source of energy. Another way, they became contaminated, and began to throw out a detrimental energy, which degenerated, and degenerated the race which was living in the caverns.

[01:12:43.820]

And according to Shaver, the Titans and the Atlans escaped the Earth, and went to another planet in these spaceships, which were similar, as I said before, to the saucers of today. And his claim is that Atlantis or Atlan or Lemuria or Mu, not simply beneath the ocean. In other words, throughout out the ages, the legend has become misconstrued, that actually what it was referring to was that the people would leave the Earth, the people of this particular continent, the engineer just brought in , go ahead with this note.

[01:13:27.440]

And it refers to the book that, I was trying to tell you about before, Ben. And the name of the book is the *Coming Race* by **Lord Lytton,** and I believe, published in London in 1891 by George Routledge & Sons. And that was the book. I didn't know that quite that much information about it. I have recalled seeing it, referred to in various publications. So what is it that's about it? Seems a perpetuation of these Deros being, degenerate beings. Not a word, of course, because according to Shaver, that there are Deros who have managed to escape the harmful ways of these mixed, as he calls them.

[01:14:08.420]

And strangely enough, the word in phonetic tongue, in other words, the tongue that the Shaver claims to have received and been the basic tongue of men due to its phonetic character lends itself to a wide, admittedly, wide interpretation. And it seems, that seems to work out just right in this phonetic spelling that is any case, but these ray nets, as Shaver called, and that these people supposedly have had control and they utilize for fiendish and diabolical purposes. In other words, they harass Sofas beings with these rays, just as a child with sort of the tantalise and end.

[01:14:52.040]

And they create the psychic, what we call psychic phenomena. They do this purely as a fiendish the very more or less, and they do create accidents, air accidents. They create all types of strange disappearances, and disturbances on the surface. And he and including and Shaver included this, the ignition of people who are sitting in their, in their living room. And they're the only thing in the whole room that are destroyed or consumed. You're familiar with that. And that's about it, Ben.

[01:15:29.300]

Did I leave anything else out that you would be curious about or anything you would like to know? No, you brough the point that I remember, I am reading the last thing Shaver wrote in a magazine that Ray Palmer published. It was, I think, a saucer issue of *Amazing Stories*, and Ray Palmer editing that one issue again, or an amazing saucer story, that's something. And Shaver had an article in which he claimed which made he the claim, obviously, again, that the saucers are actually the Deros riding around in these ships with this superior technology.

[01:16:05.960]

There's one thing, I'd like to know is why do they just bother harassing them? Why don't they just, I mean, they're so superior and dangerous and diabolical. Why don't they just take back the surface of the planet again? Well, probably their conditioning, their environment, they are accustomed to it. Actually, their cavern world would be to them, when our when our world is to us. Strangely enough, one point, I did forget them. The Shaver claims that the saucers that we see today are not here for the betterment of humanity.

[01:16:34.370]

They are not here to help anyone. They are here. They are from other planets, plundering the mechanism, this wonderful mechanisms which are in the caves. Other words, they are here to take these mechanisms back to their own planet. They are plundering the kids. And what's is that Shaver claims. What I think we should do at this time Dominic, is explain to our listeners the details of this texts that you intend to conduct. Well, John, before I go into the actual details, I would like to relate a little text.

[01:17:08.750]

Augie and myself conducted a few years back, and it was in reference to Adamski's book. Now, in Adamski's book, there was a, plate, a photographic plate which supposedly was thrown out of the saucer in which Adamski picked up. And he claimed that this platc, whcn it was developed, had an odd diagram of this comet, and it had this strange writing, now we happen to find this writing was similar to Urdu, which is a Hindu form of writing.

[01:17:49.340]

So Augie, and I sat down, and we were politically, and we decided that the Hindu into phonetic terms, and then we took the Hindu, and we put it into the Shaver alphabet, Mantong that Shaver called. And we derived from this translation a strange message, which I think Augie has more or less memorized since them. Do you recall the message, Augie? The message was John, would you and all men stay away this integrating power whose source of energy will destroy life. On another way, more or less, let's keep away from the atomic powers that properly. Probably that's about the way I now you recalled at the time.

[01:18:36.140]

It took us about eight hours to do the job, and that was to double check ourselves, actually. Now, what I would like to do if the listeners have a pencil and paper is ready. I would like to give them the phonetic version of Mantong, which was supposedly the alphabet used by the Titans and Atlants, who occupied this planet prior to 20,000 thousand years ago, now everyone is ready to go to the first letter, which is A. Our A stands for animal can be used as AM for sure.

[01:19:23.580]

In other words, M that's the letter A. Now the next letter is B, which meant in this ancient tongue, according to Shaver of course, to exist, to be. Now C. Pronounced in phonetic alphabet. CON, C-O-N, it means to see, to comprehend and to understand. The next letter is D, D-E. Which is detrimental, DIS, D-I-S, DIS for sure. Detrimental energy, concepts in that letter D. Actually, used as D-E. Then, we have E which means energy and motion.

[01:20:36.050]

G is the concept of generation to generate. H has a metaphisical connotation, even Shaver himself admitted that he couldn't quite understand the ancient concept behind the letter H. He know, he knew that has something to do with each man, each man or human, et cetera. I mean, the letter I stands for ego or self. Now, G, stands rangely enough, for a generation, but a different form of generation, it would be known to the Atlants as animal generation, and it is associated all likened to the letter G only with the difference of being an animal association to generation.

[01:21:38.770]

K stands for kinetics or the power of motion, etc. L is for life. A good word example, actually, to use in this part of the alphabet would be the word in our language: VITAL, vital, which we will use later, and we will allow the meaning. M is for men. M is for seed or spore, sort of a saucer concept. O stands for orifice, P stood for power, Q stood for Quest . R is a horror symbol, danger used as AR, which in the ancient tongue supposedly meant a dangerous quantity of the sentiment force.

[01:22:36.400]

S stands for SUN, U-S-I-S. T is the most important symbol, it stands for the force of growth, according to Shaver the actual T concept, was because of the intake of gravity, which is a little difficult to comprehend, actually. TIC, which is still working from the letter T. is the science of growth and integration. YOU stands for you as an individual. D stands for vital. Can also be used as BI, also has an animal magnetism concept attached to the letter B. W stands for will, the power of will. X is conflict, and according to

Shaver, was created to depict force lines, forcing .Y stands for the word why, W-H-Y.

[01:23:49.540]

Why that is a sort of a question or reason. C stands for zero and according to Shaver meant a quantity of T which is integrated energy neutralized by an equal quantity of D, which is more or less percentage in energy, also stands of futility. Now, I can't recall whether any of the letters there that I missed mentioned, Excite, that yeah. MC actually is zero quantity. According to Shaver, that was a C as quantity of T required by an equal quantity of D. D also could mean futility of some type.

[01:24:34.570]

According to Shaver, now, basically this this alphabet will work out in different languages, supposedly, and according to Shaver it will not work or does not work to a large degree in the romance languages, such as Italian and French. I immerse myself in these languages, and I find it extremely difficult to derive any meaning from the word that every word we try to decipher. Now, I want to go back to the word Bible just to give an idea of just how this alphabet would work.

[01:25:17.470]

Now vital is a vital force in animal magnetism VI. T is integration, A is animal. And L is life which would give a sort of a concept of power, a vital force. Actually, the work vital and the VI, which

Shaver claims practically meant vital, would stand for itself more or less so. Therefore, it's an easy way to work with. Now, Ben, have you got any ideas on this sort of alphabet, which sounds exactly like the Cabala to me, with certain letters, it sounds sounding like, I'm intrigued by these things.

[01:26:09.780]

Why is the word WHY in the letter Y? I mean, EGO or essentially I and this is something a sort of interesting to me, the identification you make between the sound of a letter and a word have a phonetic alphabet. But what it this morning phonetic that you idenfined the letter Y, with the word WHY. Shaver admitted that this is not complete. But he does claim that this will work out in certain words. Now, I have found full use of it that it does work out now whether Shaver is created.

[01:26:50.390]

But we made a generalized alphabet, which to me seems a little difficult. But one of Shaver's standing, actually. Well, I got the idea from somewhere, so I don't say he necessarily got it from the caves or that it was the original alphabet used by the people of Earth. In other words, the mother tongue of the planet. I do say that it is interesting. And, I think that if the listeners would use a few words and work this out and write one, John, in care of this station, I think that they could, we could actually have something to work with.

[01:27:32.360]

In other words, we could have a quantity of derivation, which should be interesting, don't you think so John. The point tricks me is that this is the opposite of the language that is wired to all known languages, and which is, as you point out, doesn't say why romance languages, why in the world that Do I have 26 letters? I mean, 26 Arabic lettersI couldn't understand why why wouldn't they, for instance? Well, why wouldn't may have fifty six letters in the alphabet and why shouldn't the first letter be odd, and the second letter be zepic or something like that.

[01:28:12.170]

But according to Shaver, he claims that gradually through certain subtle forces which react on humanity or surface beigns that the original language of the Titans it's again be revived. In other words, our English language is one of the closest languages to the original Mantong on planet Earth. But that would mean that the language of the ancient Phoenician. Phoenicians was almost identical with the Deros because the alphabet comes from the Phoenician mostly. Well, the Phoenicians, actually were after the cataclysm. I remember that all this Shaver mystery depends on the fact of a race of beings which inhabited the earth in pre-ataclysmic times, and are at the moment....

[01:28:53.960]

Gentlemen, I have to step out of the studio, so that I can go to the newsroom. And that I was just wondering, haveuou, do you definitely set up the set of the alphabet? John, I remember, I believe the listeners who are interested a copy of Deros, and I'm quite sure that if they derive anything, whether it's negative or positive on this, I think that, you know, what do you think should. Is there something to be analyzed here? No, more or less, John, is just a matter of interpretation.

[01:29:29.930]

Well, and what would you suggest for them to do is to send them to me? That's right John. I think we should put something on there because, I don't want to open up all these letters. I'd rather turn them over to you or to Ben, then. Do you think that as a cybernetician that this is not count on. This is not a branch of cybernatics. I am happy to figure out. I tell you what, I'm trying to figure out the way cybernatics miss out . But right now, if you send your answers to, to Ben Esquith, I ask you, you: E-S-Q-U-I-T-H, Ben Esquith, Can John Long station WFYI in New York 18 now, don't include it in a letter that you may send to me , because I will not have the opportunity of reading these.

[01:30:20.510]

These will be given to Ben, internal contact to Mr Luchesi ,and Mr. Roberts and maybe in another three or four weeks from now, we will take a few minutes to talk about it and find out what happened. You read them. Very fine. I think it would be very interesting John, to see what happens next with the word cybernetics works out very well using the Shaver alphabet. Would you tell us more about that? Please. Well, cybernetics, again, we have concepts in the alphabet, and that's the difficult part.

[01:30:51.310]

Is mental concepts. That is supposed to convey when a word is broken down. Wait a moment, as you mean, I had to step out of the studio for a couple of minutes... you said contact is this in relationship to contact Tapee. There is no, John, no connection whatsoever that I know. Very interesting stuff. But cybernetics place out would be something like the C in cybernetics, actually the C in **cybernetics** will mean to comprehend, CON, comprehend. Why was C. Concept two. Why won't be confident , comprehend. No, no.

[01:31:31.040]

It's a mental concept to say so as concept term. And C would mean to comprehend or to understand. The Y is used as a question mark. Y. Y do we have to understand. The B is we have to understand to exist these things for it to exist. E, hope I have the words forward by the way...C,Y,W & Z. In other words, why do we what do we have to say to exist?, more or less. E is energy and R naturally is the horror concept, because behind all energy, what they mean by that, is in energy there is danger.

[01:32:22.700]

And that is the way more or less Shaver himself interpreted the alphabet. In energy, there is danger. In other words, why do we have to comprehend in energy there is danger. The source of this energy is basically integrative indicated by the T, and then it finishes the word off with IC,and then an S. In other words, IC., and then we have the S concept. Just what is this? I lost it,.. fun.

[01:32:53.960]

IC some sort of energy system that works here so that we have cybernetics, which actually doesn't work out too badly in using the Shaver alphabet. Well, it may not work so badly, then what I do not understand why any of these things have to do with cybernetics, I love the thing mean. Well, the word actually, actually comes from great growth, which means... But cybernetics actually as is used today is a comprehension of the mind applied to mechanical function.

[01:33:29.180]

In other words, mind function applied to a mechanical function in order to gain knowledge. It is make correct. So, I mean it would be a proper explanation, so therefore, I guess that would be adequate. I think the Shaver explanation would be adequate also. I mean. The thing that intrigues me is because when I tried to decide the word of cybernetics, there is nothing that make sense to me, I to see why exist this energy dangerous. And it has always intrigued me is that when Shakespeare died, his Tombstone was carved in a very puzzling fashion with capital,.

Richard SHAVER

Layton Cemetery
Marion County, Arkansas

Richard
Oct 7,1907-Nov 5,1975
Dorothy
June 3,1911-Mar 14,19858

[01:34:10.260]

certain letters capitalized, certain letters not capitalized. One word broken up spaces in between them, and everyone are convinced that Shakespeare left a very important coded message tombstone. And there have been several attempts. And I think one man recently decoded the Tombstone, and really said: I was really **Marlowe** or something like that, and that the original script of Hamlet is buried in some Scottish castle. Now, S. G. Pearlmen is where America's most famous humorist once wrote one of the most brilliantly funny articles I ever read in *The New Yorker.*

[01:34:48.520]

And right after this man had tried to decipher Shakespeare's tombston, and he went to Grant's tomb, and he decided there was some hidden cipher in Grand's tomb. And it's that very, very mystifying method. Ulysses S. Grant is buried here, you know, and this is quite common, and it suggested all sorts of coded possibilities. And he worked out a system very close to a man who figured out a Texas tomb match, actually said, It was really **Marlowe**. And he worked at a system where he got the inscription on Grant's Tomb, said Robert E.

[01:35:25.940]

Lee is really buried here. Now, it is a sounding conclusion, and just as valid as the other one. And what I really want to point out is that when you look for something, you're going to find it, especially in an cryptogram. I am absolutely and I agree with you 100 percent that I don't say this is alphabet is a direct revelation to Shaver from thought records from a civilization which existed there in pre-cataclysmic times. But, I said the same thing you said. I say it's extremely interesting to work with the Shaver mystery is an intriguing mystery in itself.

[01:36:03.740]

There is a lot of information relating to the Shaver Mystery which is dangerous for people to pursue. In other words, in other words, you are in the Deros would retaliate. It is claimed that Deros have recovered, and returns. It is also claimed, we have won great science fiction writer Taylor Hansen, who, by the way, strangely enough, used to write for *Amazing Stories*. He became interested in the Shaver Mystery. And now **Taylor Hansen** disappeared while on a trip into the desert in California

[01:36:45.110]

to relocate a large border, there was some type of a border which went down into the area and according to what can be still derived from this information, Hansen described as borders, as having smooth glace sides. And I can't recall exactly if it was clear or around, and **L Tylor Hansen**, and went again to relocate it, and he was never heard from again. I'm not supposed to to certain methods of attempting Deros to show. I understood that if you're alone at night, I assure you, I don't believe in Deros, and also that if you try, you know, I've never tried it.

[01:37:34.220]

I mean, I tell the FBI that will take Deros. But I think also that if you let be another way is that if you publicly states that there are no such things as Deros, and you dare Deros to do it. Deros they do anything to you. The Deros will get rid of you in such a way to look like a normal accident. Well, I wouldn't know Ben so far. I've been talking about Deros for quite a while, and you never alleviated one.

[01:38:02.630]

And a little later in the program, I am carrying on my person an actual photograph of a Dero of what is claimed to be a Dero. I got this one here. I think the world has possibilities of being, a being from a cavern. It is the same thing. I doubt it, Ben. There is the only one of this kind in existence, it is is the only one of that type. But I also have home a grain for a supposed Dero, which is quite interesting.

[01:38:39.140]

Well, I think this photograph, as soon as we showed, Ben, I think that he will change or that I don't know. A Dero is a type of microscopic micro microscopic worm is that what you referred. No, a Dero derived the name from detrimental RO or detrimental ROBOT. No, and actually it was the cause. It was caused by this detrimental energy, that negative energy which began to eliminate from the sun. So actually tearing down into the Shaver Alphabet or not the Shaver alphabet, I should say, the alphabet of the Titans, it would be known as **Mantong**.

[01:39:18.680]

And using **Mantong** to derive the meaning of Dero, we would have detrimental energy horror source would be the concept derived from **Mantong**. Dominick, Are you familiar with the science fiction classic of **E. van Vogt** ? No, not particularly. I recall reading it. I don't recall the story. The context itself. It is one of the most brilliant concepts that van **Vogt** created with sounds very familiar, so very similar to the detrimental energy concept and this myth I had a different name for.

[01:39:58.580]

It was that a super civilization invented a type of mechanism called DISTORTER. And if this story was something that could take over any machine, and interfere with its function, DISTORTER could transport people instantly, through time and space. In fact, they used them as elevators. You know, you walk into an elevator on the ground floor, and you were transported to the 24th floor. It wasn't a real elevator, didn't go up and down through the elevator shaft. It just transported you through time and space. Also, can transport you to the planet Venus.

[01:40:32.090]

It also did certain things. The people control their mind and all the rest of it. And this is a very brilliant science fiction concept, was never claimed to be true. But it sounds, it sounds like coming from the same general source. Shaver himself claimed that certain people were in rapport or put in this way, contacted by E.S.P with Teros, which are the good Deros, or in other words, Integrarors He claimed that the works of **Merrritt**, and you have read Merritt, the moon pool, the ship from this time, he claimed that Merritt was in contact with the Tero who resided in the caverns, and that many of the stories contain some of the basic, basic truths of the ancients.

[01:41:31.430]

Now, it became in history in mythology. We have only the references to the elders, the old ones. We have references to oracles, which as a rule resided in caverns or caves. It always seems it is always a reference to the deaths, the realms of darkness, as they are referred to, we have references to the inferno. We have references, even today, of a primitive great god **Erichthonius**, wich supposed was born out of a hole in the ground. What is the source of calling the organized crime on the surface today, The Underworld?.

[01:42:10.570]

I mean, you see, we have these various references even to this day. And after all, I mean, Ben, there does seem to be actually, the Shaver Mystery proof upon proof of things to build up. Shaver predicted, and I can't recall the exact event. I can't recall the exact particle. Shaver not only predicted, but he came out with concepts of gravitation, and he claimed that gravitation was actually a force, an infadrift. What? An **ETHER DRIF**. I don't know what that what he meant was that there are these particles which are dispersed, these particles traveling at fantastic velocities, which have a tendency, in some way, to become to change from a pure wave form into a corpuscular form of matter.

[01:43:02.570]

And by their friction of penetration to matter as we know, it creates a weak gravity. In other words, these particles are actually gravitational particles. And I certainly, I am now looking at the molecular weight, is responsible for gravity?. Ben, how can you misconstrue my intention? I am only stating what Shaver said. I am not in no way, stating my own personal belief or opinions in gravitational field. Well, I would I would find in relativity, but I don't think I humble submitt that Shaver was well, over his head. Well, strangely enough Ben, you find that Shaver's predicted that in a short time a smaller particle of matter of a particular type would be found.

[01:43:55.850]

I cannot recall the exact naming attributed to it. I cannot recall the exact way he said it would be found. But strangely enough, it happened. As Shaver said, I can do it right now. I suppose over the next six months, two **MESON** particles will be found, if they find one every three months. Yeah, but you are **Ben Isquith**. You are a cybernetician. You work as a more or less a scientist. Shaver was not a cybernetician..

[01:44:22.340]

He was not a scientist. Well, he was a wellder working in a shipyard,he was a welder in a shipyard. Then again, we have to take Shaver's position. We have to take his attitude, his type of person. Shaver, from what I can gather, I never met the man personally from what I could gather.... Yes, you have never seen Shaver?. Definitely. Definitely, definitely. I'll tell you, a couple of people that have met Shaver, to my knowledge. Curtis Fuller, the head editor of the *Fate* **magazine**.

[01:44:58.630]

Yes. Oh, yeah. I remember that during the coffee break, he told us that Shaver, this maybe is news to you Dominik, Shaver was a pretty good writer. And he was a sports writer at one time, and eventually went to science fiction. You know that, I knew that he was some form of writer, John. But I mean, just how good he was or how successful, I don't know. Why would a confident writer turned over to Palmer scrap paper with little notations on the back of an envelope and things like that?

[01:45:37.320]

Right. Well, if as you said before, John. You learn that he was getting, as I said, that he was getting the messages through the welding machine, and you came up with a very good point as he was receiving these messages, he would have to use whatever he had on hand. And that would be describing these messages onto the backs of envelopes probably at the time, even while he was getting the messages, he wasn't attributing too much basic facts to him.

[01:46:06.200]

He wasn't actually thinking about it too much. He was probably just packing sheets of scrap paper, and envelopes, and sending him in to Palmer just for the sheer joy more or less. Sometime ago, you know, they published a book, I think it was in Cairo that he found the world, and that book with all of that by the author, Richard S. Shaver, that should be interested. So then you should know that that was actually Shaver who wrote that book.

[01:46:38.990]

You know what Shaver do, I don't know what Shaver do with you. Oh, I wish it was Ben, it was Ben. And they also remember him and Palmer put out a book called *I Remember Lemuria* and *The Return of Sathanas,* which was by Richard S. Shaver, but is definitely a Palmer's contribution, which made it readable. And that was put out by Vintage Books in 1948. So, actually there was hardcover books published, but they were in limited quantities.

[01:47:12.620]

And actually, I don't think the Shaver today is doing any writing, from what I can gather from. What is he doing? Welding? That, I don't know, John. I know he lives in a very different section of the country. Which part of the country the country? Wisconsin,

Wisconsin, yeap. Wisconsin in Amherst. Is there a possibility and I'm not trying to be facetious, but is there a possibility that maybe Palmer has Shaver working for, at the plant?

[01:47:44.330]

You know, he has a printing plant. Gee, I don't know, John. I would not inquire Palmer as Shaver has a particular occupation at this time. But I do know that one of the things that seems to be the strongest point of the whole argument, what we recall in this discussion, is the fact that a magazine that has boosted its circulation to one hundred and eighty five thousand copies per month for a science fiction magazine, remember, just by including the **Shaver Mystery**. Now, the contention is the pressure was put on this magazine by *Amazing Stories* by a group of science fiction writers led by a 17 year old boy at the time.

[01:48:31.780]

No, actually, I don't think that was the excuse that we used, but I don't think that any actually the circulation was increased to such a vast degree that I don't think the science fiction group with a majority of buyers of the magazine any longer. Do you mean do you mean to imply Dominik? That a 17 year old boy. Would carry so much weight, that the publichers Ziff-Davis, would decide to discontinue the publishing of Shaver of the show, the mystery, when it boosted the circulation up to a hundred and eighty five thousand.

[01:49:17.890]

That's just what I was getting into, John. You know, I don't think that's a small minority group like that. What could cause a publisher to drop the magazine or the drop the **Shaver Mystery** would should say, because I know myself. I spoke to news dealers, and news dealers told me that as soon as the Shaver Mystery was dropped from the magazine, that the magazines were moving off the shelves, as they were previous to that. Now, what do you think about what, you're implying something?

[01:49:46.830]

Nothing. I'm not implying, John. I'm just wondering, what is it?. I like to know what, because when I made that statement before about the FBI investigating Shaver, and, and then John , jumped on my neck, let me finish. I never jumped. Cybernetically. And that what they told him, actually is Palmer's way, it is one fact which made it difficult to grasp the mystery, mystery, the same factor. And the other part of the sentence, convinced Shaver's of the reality of flying saucers, the same factor.

[01:50:27.670]

In other words, whatever these men told him, convinced Shaver, of the reality of saucers. So there is definitely, you said that is a silence group. What do you mean? Silence group blocking people talking, keeping certain facts away from people , not only what we call technology away from people, but keeping certain facts away from people? Well, I think **Major Keyhoe** is under this impression.

[01:50:58.510]

For **Major Keyhoe** is under this impression. **Major Keyhoe** is under the impression that certain branch of the government. You are not referred to the government. No, I'm not referring to the government. I say that there are forces on this planet, which we know little of. I remembered. When you say Marxist, are you talking about human beings now? I don't know, John. I just say some type of, can be called, metaphysical concept we could call some type of a metaphysical force, brought down to the level of a human being.

[01:51:26.860]

I don't know, John, but I do remember one thing during our investigation. That's on, on my self on the **Bender Mystery**. I remember saying to Bender, I said to Bender I said, is it possible that we are owned by someone or something? And he turned white. Did you recall that time? And I stopped, and I said, it is possible that we are owned by someone or something that is quite a fantastic concept that there would be forces which would withhold men from achieving what may be some type of cosmic heritage, which we are entitled them. I just lowered the temperature in room this to 20 degrees for a region of my spine.

[01:52:13.750]

But I'll tell you, I hope. What was this, power. What happened? But we talked lot about the powers , John, that maybe balancing. Maybe powers that be, which acts in a very subtle manner, probably acting on some of the more principle forces of life in general, which are throttling the human mind to the degree where eventually it will destroy itself. I don't know. I hope that there is not going to do any silencing, that they don't start on me, until I get through with a couple of business right now.

[01:52:50.830]

And some of his relatives have said those who no longer want to be associated with the Lucchesi family, they claim that Dominick is possibly a direct descendant of the D'Rose, Benjamin Fisklet, the cybernetician. Gentleman, the word sounds the seven oh three, the seven oh four. And also he works on the 650. And according to some of his fans, he should be in seven oh one. That's at school. You know, I say that we've had as engineers and they're very, very competent engineers.

END

A Dictionary of The Shaver Mystery Discussion On Long John Nebel PartyLine, 1958

2nd Washington Sighting- The 1952 Washington, D.C. UFO incident, also known as the Washington flap, the Washington National Airport Sightings, or the Invasion of Washington,[1] was a series of unidentified flying object reports from July 12 to July 29, 1952, over Washington, D.C. The most publicized sightings took place on consecutive weekends, July 19–20 and July 26–27. UFO historians called the incident "the climax of the 1952 (UFO) flap".

Atlans- As an adjective, Atlantean (or Atlantian) means "of or pertaining to Atlas or Atlantis".

Atlantis- Atlantis (Ancient Greek: Ἀτλαντὶς νῆσος, "island of Atlas") is a fictional island mentioned in an allegory on the hubris of nations in Plato's works Timaeus and Critias, where it represents the antagonist naval power that besieges "Ancient Athens", the pseudo-historic embodiment of Plato's ideal state in The Republic. In the story, Athens repels the Atlantean attack unlike any other nation of the known world, supposedly bearing witness to the superiority of Plato's concept of a state. The story concludes with Atlantis falling out of favor with the deities and submerging into the Atlantic Ocean. Despite its minor importance in Plato's work, the Atlantis story has had a considerable impact on literature. The allegorical aspect of Atlantis was taken up in utopian works of several Renaissance writers, such as Francis Bacon's New Atlantis and Thomas More's Utopia. On the other hand, nineteenth-century amateur scholars misinterpreted Plato's narrative as historical tradition, most famously Ignatius L. Donnelly in his Atlantis: The Antediluvian World. Plato's vague indications of the time of the events—more than 9,000 years before his time—and the alleged location of Atlantis—"beyond the Pillars of Hercules"—has led to much pseudoscientific speculation. As a consequence, Atlantis has become a byword for any and all supposed advanced prehistoric lost civilizations and continues to inspire contemporary fiction, from comic books to films.

Benjamin Fisklet- the cybernetician.

Ben Isquith- An skeptic invited by Long John Nebel to his program. The cybernetician in this radio broadcast. However, at the same time, there was a painter called Ben Isquith. It is hard to tell if both are the same person.

Bender Mystery- Referred to the "Men In Black" incident. According to ufologists, Men In Black, popularly identified as MIB, are ultra-secret agents associated with the FBI, CIA, or an unnamed covert federal department which seek out and thwart those individuals probing too close to the truth behind UFOs. Some ufologists alarmingly postulate that the MIB are actually not of this Earth.

Blavatsky-Helena Petrovna Blavatsky (Russian: Еле́на Петро́вна Блава́тская, Yelena Petrovna Blavatskaya, often known as Madame Blavatsky; née von Hahn; 12 August [O.S. 31 July] 1831 – 8 May 1891) was a controversial Russian occultist, philosopher, and author who co-founded the Theosophical Society in 1875. She gained an international following as the leading theoretician of Theosophy, the esoteric movement that the society promoted.

Colin- Colin Henry Wilson (26 June 1931 – 5 December 2013) was an English writer, philosopher and novelist. He also wrote widely on true crime, mysticism and the paranormal, eventually writing more than a hundred books.[Wilson called his philosophy "new existentialism" or "phenomenological existentialism", and maintained his life work was "that of a philosopher, and (his) purpose to create a new and optimistic existentialism.

Cybernetician- Ben Isquith
Cybernetics-control theory as it is applied to complex systems. Cybernetics is associated with models in which a monitor compares what is happening to a system at various sampling times with some standard of what should be happening, and a controller adjusts the system's behaviour accordingly.

Deros - Detrimental Robot.

Dominik Lucchesi- guest of LJN to his programs.

E. van Vogt-Alfred Elton van Vogt (/væn voʊt/; April 26, 1912 – January 26, 2000) was a Canadian-born science fiction author. His fragmented, bizarre narrative style influenced later science fiction writers, notably Philip K. Dick. He was one of the most popular and influential practitioners of science fiction in the mid-twentieth century, the genre's so-called Golden Age, and one of the most complex.

Edward Bulwer- Edward George Earle Lytton Bulwer-Lytton.

ETHER DRIFT:
Graham, Roger. P (1947). *WHAT MAN CAN IMAGINE. Is there an Ether Drift?* Amazing Stories, June, 1947. Pp. 152-158.

Erichthonius- was an early king of ancient Athens in Greek mythology, and it was believed that he was autochthonous (born of the soil).

Fate- is aU.S. magazine about paranormal phenomena. Fate was co-founded in 1948 by Raymond A. Palmer (editor of *Amazing Stories*) and Curtis Fuller. Fate magazine is the longest-running magazine devoted to the paranormal. Promoted as "the world's leading magazine of the paranormal", it has published expert opinions and personal experiences relating to UFOs, psychic abilities, ghosts and hauntings, cryptozoology, alternative medicine, divination methods, belief in the survival of personality after death, Fortean phenomena, predictive dreams, mental telepathy, archaeology, warnings of death, and other paranormal topics.

Harlan Ellison- Harlan Jay Ellison (May 27, 1934 – June 28, 2018) was an American writer, known for his prolific and influential work in New Wave speculative fiction, and for his outspoken, combative personality. Robert Bloch, the author of Psycho, described Ellison as "the only living organism I know whose natural habitat is hot water". His published works include more than 1,700 short stories, novellas, screenplays, comic book scripts, teleplays, essays, and a wide range of criticism covering literature, film, television, and print media. Some of his best-known works include the Star Trek episode "The City on the Edge of Forever" (he subsequently wrote a book about the experience that includes his original screenplay), his A Boy and His Dog cycle, and his short stories "I Have No Mouth, and I Must Scream" and "'Repent, Harlequin!' Said the Ticktockman". He was also editor and anthologist for Dangerous Visions (1967) and Again, Dangerous Visions (1972). Ellison won numerous awards, including multiple Hugos, Nebulas, and Edgars.

Judge Crater - Joseph Force Crater (January 5, 1889 – disappeared August 6, 1930, declared legally dead June 6, 1939) was a New York State Supreme Court Justice who vanished amid political scandal. He was last seen leaving a restaurant on West 45th Street in Manhattan and entered popular culture as one of the most mysterious missing persons cases of the twentieth century. Despite massive publicity, the case was never solved and was officially closed forty years after he disappeared. Crater's disappearance fueled public disquiet about New York City corruption and was a factor in the downfall of the Tammany Hall political machine.

Kenneth Arnold-The Kenneth Arnold UFO sighting occurred on June 24, 1947, when private pilot Kenneth Arnold claimed that he saw a string of nine, shiny unidentified flying objects flying past Mount Rainier at speeds that Arnold estimated at a minimum of 1,200 miles an hour (1,932 km/hr). This was the first post-War sighting in the United States that garnered nationwide news coverage and is credited with being the first of the modern era of UFO sightings, including numerous reported sightings over the next two to three weeks. Arnold's description of the objects also led to the press quickly coining the terms flying saucer and flying disc as popular descriptive terms for UFOs.

Lemuria- is a continent that, according to a disproved scientific theory put forward in 1864 by zoologist Philip Sclater, was located in, and subsequently sank beneath, the Indian Ocean. The theory was proposed as an explanation for the presence of lemur fossils in both Madagascar and India, but not in Africa or the Middle East.

Lytton-Edward George Earle Lytton Bulwer-Lytton, 1st Baron Lytton, PC (25 May 1803 – 18 January 1873) was an English writer and politician. He served as a Whig member of Parliament from 1831 to 1841 and a Conservative from 1851 to 1866. He was Secretary of State for the Colonies from June 1858 to June 1859, choosing Richard Clement Moody as founder of British Columbia. He declined the Crown of Greece in 1862 after King Otto abdicated. He was created Baron Lytton of Knebworth in 1866. His marriage to the writer Rosina Bulwer Lytton broke down. Her detention in an insane asylum provoked a public outcry. Bulwer-Lytton's works sold and paid him well. He coined the phrases "the great unwashed", "pursuit of the almighty dollar", "the pen is mightier than the sword", and "dweller on the threshold", and the opening phrase "It was a dark and stormy night." Yet his standing declined and he is little read today.

Major Keyhoe- Donald Edward Keyhoe (June 20, 1897 – November 29, 1988) was an American Marine Corps naval aviator, writer of many aviation articles and stories in a variety of leading publications, and manager of the promotional tours of aviation pioneers, especially of Charles Lindbergh. In the 1950s he became well known as a UFO researcher, arguing that the U.S. Government should conduct research in UFO matters, and should release all its UFO files. Jerome Clark writes that "Keyhoe was widely regarded as the leader in the field" of ufology in the 1950s and early to mid-1960s.

MANTONG- Mantong Alphabet, a supposed prehistoric proto-language spoken in Atlantis and Lemuria.

Marlowe- Christopher Marlowe, also known as Kit Marlowe (/ˈmɑːrloʊ/; baptised 26 February 1564 – 30 May 1593), was an English playwright, poet and translator of the Elizabethan era. Modern scholars count Marlowe among the most famous of the Elizabethan playwrights; based upon the "many imitations" of his play Tamburlaine, they consider him to have been the foremost dramatist in London in the years just before his mysterious early death.

Men In Black-See Bender Mystery.

Merritt-Abraham Grace Merritt (January 20, 1884 – August 21, 1943) – known by his byline, A. Merritt was an American Sunday magazine editor and a writer of fantastic fiction.

MESON- Meson, any member of a family of subatomic particles composed of a quark and an antiquark. Mesons are sensitive to the strong force, the fundamental interaction that binds the components of the nucleus by governing the behaviour of their constituent quarks . Predicted theoretically in 1935 by the Japanese physicist Yukawa Hideki, the existence of mesons was confirmed in 1947 by a team led by the English physicist Cecil Frank Powell with the discovery of the pi-meson (pion) in cosmic-ray particle interactions.

Mu- A legendary lost continent. It is a term introduced by Augustus Le Plongeon, who used the "Land of Mu" as an alternative name for Atlantis. It was subsequently popularized as an alternative term for the hypothetical land of Lemuria by James Churchward, who asserted that Mu was located in the Pacific Ocean before its destruction. Archaeologists assign assertions about Mu to the category of pseudoarchaeology. The place of Mu in literature has been discussed in detail in Lost Continents (1954) by L. Sprague de Camp. Geologists dismiss the existence of Mu and the lost continent of Atlantis as physically impossible, arguing that a continent can neither sink nor be destroyed in the short period of time asserted in legends and folklore and literature about these places. Theories about Lemuria and other sunken lands became unscientific when, in the 1960s, the scientific community finally accepted Alfred Wegener's theory of continental drift, presented back in 1912, according to which, in particular, the similarity of living organisms in different parts of the world is explained. According to this theory, all land in the ancient past of the Earth was combined into one supercontinent – Pangaea.

Ray Palmer- Raymond Arthur Palmer (August 1, 1910 – August 15, 1977[1]) was an American author and editor, best known as editor of Amazing Stories from 1938 through 1949, when he left publisher Ziff-Davis to publish and edit Fate Magazine, and eventually many other magazines and books through his own publishing houses, including Amherst Press and Palmer Publications. In addition to magazines such as Mystic, Search, and Flying Saucers, he published or republished numerous spiritualist books, including Oahspe: A New Bible, as well as several books related to flying saucers, including The Coming of the Saucers, co-written by Palmer with Kenneth Arnold. Palmer was also a prolific author of science fiction and fantasy stories, many of which were published under pseudonyms.

Richard Shaver- Richard Sharpe Shaver (October 8, 1907 Berwick, Pennsylvania – November 5, 1975 Summit, Arkansas) was an American writer and artist. Shaver's stories continued to appear in Amazing after Howard Browne replaced Ray Palmer as editor. Even after his work fell out of favor with Amazing readers, Ray Palmer continued to publish Shaver in other genre magazines. A special issue of Fantastic devoted to the "Shaver Mystery" was published in 1958. He achieved notoriety in the years following World War II as the author of controversial stories that were printed in science fiction magazines (primarily Amazing Stories), in which he claimed that he had had personal experience of a sinister, ancient civilization that harbored fantastic technology in caverns under the earth. The controversy stemmed from the claim by Shaver, and his editor and publisher Ray Palmer, that Shaver's writings, while presented in the guise of fiction, were fundamentally.

Sanskrit- A classical language of South Asia belonging to the Indo-Aryan branch of the Indo-European languages.

Taylor Hansen- L. Tylor Hansen-L. (Lucile) Taylor Hansen (November 30, 1897 – May 1976) was a writer of science fiction popular science articles and books who used a male writing persona for the early part of her career. She is the author of eight short stories, nearly sixty nonfiction articles popularizing anthropology and geology, and three nonfiction books. The Science Fiction and Fantasy Hall of Fame inducted him in 1999.
Titans- In the Greek mythology, the Titans were a race of powerful giant deities (bigger than the gods who would replace them) that ruled during the legendary and long Golden Age. Their role as Elder gods being overthrown by a race of younger gods, the Olympians (led by Zeus).

Vril-Vril is form of energy mentioned by Edward Bulwer-Lytton in his novel The Coming Race. The Vril is an "all-permeating fluid" that serves as latent source of energy. The novel describes subterranean race, the "Vril-ya", who where able to master this extraordinary force through training of their will. The vril is a neutral force that be used either as an agent of destruction or as a healing substance.H. P. Blavatsky said: "The name vril may be a fiction; the Force itself is a fact doubted as little in India as the existence itself of their Rishis, since it is mentioned in all the secret works." This force is equated to akasha by Mahatma K. H. As Mme. Blavatsky stated, this force can be mastered by human beings: Electricity is a most powerful force not fully known to modern science, yet used very much. The nervous, physical, and mental systems of man acting together are able to produce the same force exactly, and in a finer as well as subtler way and to as great a degree as the most powerful dynamo, so that the force might be used to kill, to alter, to move, or otherwise change any object or condition. This is the "vril" described by Bulwer Lytton in his Coming Race.

News Paper Articles on the Shaver Mystery

Then There's Flying Saucers

WITH THE OVERLOAD of political news today, not too much is heard of the elusive flying saucers.

But what a pleasant break it is to hear of a sighting and to again start the exciting game of fathoming what the darn things are!

BACK IN THE DAYS of World War II, there was a Pittsburgh man who mentioned flying saucer types of craft in his many science-fiction writings. This was Richard S. Shaver, a welder in the Pittsburgh district. Shaver had submitted a manuscript, supposedly true, to Ray Palmer, then editor of the temendously popular science-fiction magazine. "Amazing Stores." This paper dealt with a race of people who lived underground and who were the remaining citizens of a long-lost civilization that were classed among the Atlanteans and ancient Titans.

ature adulterated by claims of
fact.

Since then, the question still
remains, why did "Amazing
Stories" drop a series that had
made the publisher a half million dollars and was still able
to make more? Or did the flying
saucer subject seem more pro-
fitable to publishers? Many writers have made a "killing" on
the flying disk subject.

RICHARD S. SHAVER later
moved to Amherst, Wisconsin,
and not too much has been heard
of him lately. But he did stir up

quite a storm with his "Dero"
and a similar, but friendly race
called the "Tero." Both were
underground denizens of this
planet, according to Shaver.

There is only one portion of
the Shaver Mystery that might
be accepted as fact; something
or someone is certainly "bug-
ging" the people of this old
planet Earth these days. It may
be "ray machines" or a new
kind of virus-like a "jitters"
germ.

Folks just don't get along like
they used to.

Quad-City Times
Davenport, Iowa
14 May 1972, Sun. Page 106

The Underworld Kingdom Of Richard Shaver

In the March, 1945, issue of Amazing Stories, editor Ray Palmer introduced the now famous Shaver Mystery. Richard Shaver, a young welder, claimed to remember a life among a civilization which inhabited a vast, underground cave system deep in the bowels of the earth. Later, Shaver changed this claim of a past-life to an assertion that he had lived just recently with the cave-dwellers.

It is Richard Shaver's contention that in prehistoric times, when our solar system was young, earth was inhabited by a race of cosmic super-beings who had come here from another solar system. Although the Elder Race were not truly immortal, they had discovered secrets of longevity. This, together with their highly developed scientific technology, caused them to be regarded as gods by the primitive and unsophisticated humans. The Elder Race pos-sessed fantastic mechanical devices capable of projecting three dimensional images, extracting or implanting thoughts into others' minds, scanning over great distances, curing diseases, producing food and clothing and killing and destroying life when necessary.

After a time the Elder Race began to notice that the sun contained detrimental rays which were shortening their lifespan by promoting premature aging. In order to escape the harmful rays of the sun, some of the Elder Race left earth for a more suitable planet, while others entered deep, underground caverns and began to carve a fantastic underworld kingdom, using their ray guns to disintegrate rock. Soon they had constructed powerful machines which could duplicate the health-giving rays of the sun, while excluding the detrimental radioactivity.

But then, according to Shaver, something went very wrong with these machines, and they began to emit a harmful radiation which destroyed a portion of their brains. This radiation produced a dangerous form of hereditary insanity, and it affected many of the Elder Race. These unfortunate people became Dero, which meant a detrimental or degenerate being. Those who remained unaffected called themselves the Tero, for the T was a symbol of good in the religion of the Elder Race.

The threat to mankind, according to Richard Shaver, is that the Dero, who sadistically enjoy interfering with human, surface affairs, are becoming more numerous than the gentle Tero. Also, both have access to the vast technology of the Elder Race, and the increase in strength among the Dero signifies an increasingly destructive application of these technology. Those of us on the surface, of course, would bear the brunt of this destruction.

The Shaver Mystery continues to elicit alleged first-hand accounts from others who claim to have known the Tero or the Dero, and the furor the mystery originally set off among science fiction and Fortean buffs continues to break out in periodic brush fires. But until the Tero or the Dero openly surface, the Shaver Mystery must remain unsolved.

Edmonton Journal (Edmonton, Alberta, Canada)
15 Feb 2001, Thu •Page 25

The madman, the midget and the giants

PETER CARLSON
The Washington Post
WASHINGTON

Deep in the bowels of the earth, a mutant race of malevolent beings keeps thousands of kidnapped humans as slaves and sex toys before ultimately eating them.

At least that's what Richard S. Shaver believed, and who cares that he was a raving lunatic? He had a good editor, who happened to be a hunchbacked midget, who turned Shaver's demented screeds into some of the most popular pulp magazine stories of the 1940s.

I'm not making this up. It's way too weird to be fiction. The whole strange story is recounted in the current issue of *Outre* magazine, a smart, fun, profusely illustrated quarterly devoted to the history of B-movies, pulp magazines and classic pinup girls. *Outre* is six years old, but I'd never seen it until I stumbled upon the latest issue at a newsstand. As I read Bruce Wright's *Fear Down Below: The Curious History of the Shaver Mystery*, my jaw dropped and I stood transfixed. It's the most bizarre nonfiction story I've

Stories.

One day in 1943, one of Palmer's assistants tossed a letter from a reader into the wastebasket, muttering about "crackpots." Curious, Palmer picked the epistle out of the trash. It was from Shaver, a then-unknown ex-hobo and construction worker who wrote that he'd discovered "Mantong," the lost language of Atlantis, which he claimed was the basis of all earthly tongues. Palmer printed the letter and it drew a considerable response from readers who said they recognized Mantong phraseology in various foreign languages.

When Palmer wrote to Shaver, asking how he'd discovered Mantong, Shaver bombarded the editor with long, semi-coherent letters, explaining that he'd been working at a Detroit auto plant when his welding gun began suddenly picking up the thoughts of his co-workers. That was weird

read in years and a delightful look into the hidden history of American magazines.

The story begins with Raymond A. Palmer, a four-foot-tall hunchback from Milwaukee who spent his sickly childhood reading science fiction. He founded a sci-fi fan club and published a sci-fi fanzine and in 1938, at age 28, was hired to edit a dying Chicago pulp sci-fi mag called *Amazing*

enough, but then the welding gun started broadcasting the sounds of a secret torture session held in a cavern deep in the earth.

Shaver also sent Palmer *A Warning to Future Man*, a 10,000-word manuscript detailing the secret history of our planet. Thousands of years ago, Earth, then called Lemuria, was occupied by a race of immortal giants, Shaver wrote. But then the sun began emitting poison particles that drove the giants underground, where they mutated into ugly, evil beings called Dero, who kidnap, rape and devour humans.

Your average editor would have tossed Shaver's ravings. Not Palmer. He rewrote the manuscript into a piece called *I Remember Lemuria!*, which he billed as fact and published in the March 1945 issue of *Amazing Stories*.

Richard S. Shaver

The issue sold out and drew hundreds of letters from readers. For the next four years, Palmer kept rewriting Shaver's sadistic fantasies, illustrating them with wonderfully lurid covers that featured scantily clad women menaced by Shaver's Dero demons.

"The result," writes Wright, "is an unforgettable blend of high-flying imagination with curiously homely touches, as when we encounter a highly intelligent snail-centaur named Hank."

Shaver's stories helped boost *Amazing Stories*' circulation from 27,000 to 185,000. Soon there was a Shaver cult, complete with a fan club and monthly fanzine.

The Atlantic Monthly and *Life* published stories on the strange phenomenon.

Shaver, who was probably a paranoid schizophrenic, believed that his writings were simple fact. It's hard to tell what Palmer thought. At one point, he claimed that Shaver's stuff might be "at least 25 percent true."

In the '50s, the two men parted ways. Palmer left *Amazing Stories* to publish *Fate*, which achieved fame by touting the existence of flying saucers. (*Fate* is still publishing and still touting UFOs;

Amazing Stories lasted in various incarnations until last year.)

Meanwhile, Shaver published his own mag, *Shaver Mystery Magazine*, which appeared only sporadically. Later, he claimed he'd discovered detailed written records of Lemuria inside rocks he found on the Wisconsin prairie, but for some reason scientists didn't believe him. In the '60s, the two teamed up on a magazine called the *Hidden World* but it never caught on, possibly because it published Shaver's writings unedited. America apparently wasn't ready for prose like this: "Life is a scream in the face of a bright madness, then! Life is a silly sound like a death rattle from an insane clown dying in the night, then!"

Both men died in the '70s, and we'll no doubt never see their like again. But in an era when magazines are edited by timid souls who make editorial decisions based on demographic data and focus groups, it's pleasing to recall that at least one editor once achieved success by rewriting the ravings of a madman.

(Outre is available at full-service newsstands for $7.95 or by subscription for $30 a year at P.O. Box 1900, Evanston, Ill. 60204.)

Democrat and Chronicle
Rochester, New York
16 Feb 2001, Fri • Page 21

Wild writer meets hunchbacked editor

THE WASHINGTON POST

PETER CARLSON

Deep in the bowels of the earth, a mutant race of malevolent beings keeps thousands of kidnapped humans as slaves and sex toys before ultimately eating them.

At least that's what Richard S. Shaver believed, and who cares that he was a raving lunatic? He had a good editor, who happened to be a hunchbacked midget, who turned Shaver's demented screeds into some of the most popular pulp magazine stories of the 1940s.

I'm not making this up. It's way too weird to be fiction. The whole strange story is recounted in the current issue of *Outre* magazine, a smart, fun, profusely illustrated quarterly devoted to the history of B-movies, pulp magazines and classic pinup girls. *Outre* is six years old, but I'd never seen it until I stumbled upon the latest issue at a newsstand. As I read Bruce Wright's *Fear Down Below: The Curious History of the Shaver Mystery*, my jaw dropped, and I stood transfixed. It's the most bizarre nonfiction story I've read in years and a delightful look into the hidden history of American magazines.

The story begins with Raymond A. Palmer, a 4-foot-tall hunchback from Milwaukee who spent his sickly childhood reading science fiction. He founded a sci-fi fan club and published a sci-fi fanzine and in 1938, at age 28, was hired to edit a dying Chicago pulp sci-fi mag called *Amazing Stories*.

One day in 1943, one of Palmer's assistants tossed a letter from a reader into the wastebasket, muttering about "crackpots." Curious, Palmer picked the epistle out of the trash. It was from Shaver, a then-unknown ex-hobo and construction worker who wrote that he'd

108

discovered "Mantong," the lost language of Atlantis, which he claimed was the basis of all Earthly tongues. Palmer printed the letter and it drew a considerable response from readers who said they recognized Mantong phraseology in various foreign languages.

When Palmer wrote to Shaver, asking how he'd discovered Mantong, Shaver bombarded the editor with long, semi-coherent letters, explaining that he'd been working at a Detroit auto plant when his welding gun suddenly began picking up the thoughts of his co-workers. That was weird enough, but then the welding gun started broadcasting the sounds of a secret torture session held in a cavern deep in the Earth.

Shaver also sent Palmer *A Warning to Future Man,* a 10,000-word manuscript detailing the secret history of our planet. Thousands of years ago, Earth, then called Lemuria, was occupied by a race of immortal giants, Shaver wrote. But then the sun began emitting poison particles that drove the giants underground, where they mutated into ugly, evil beings called Dero, who kidnap, rape and devour humans.

Your average editor would have tossed Shaver's ravings. Not Palmer. He rewrote the manuscript into a piece called *I Remember Lemuria!,* which he billed as fact and published in the March 1945 issue of *Amazing Stories.*

The issue sold out and drew hundreds of letters from readers. For the next four years, Palmer kept rewriting Shaver's sadistic fantasies, illustrating them with wonderfully lurid covers that featured scantily clad women menaced by Shaver's Dero demons.

"The result," writes Wright, "is an unforgettable blend of high-flying imagination with curiously homely touches, as when we encounter a highly intelligent snail-centaur named Hank."

Shaver's stories helped boost

'Outre'

Outre is available at full-service newsstands for $5.95 or by subscription for $20 a year at P.O. Box 1900, Evanston, IL 60204.

Amazing Stories' circulation from 27,000 to 185,000. Soon there was a Shaver cult, complete with a fan club and monthly fanzine. *The Atlantic Monthly* and *Life* published stories on the strange phenomenon.

Shaver, who was probably a paranoid schizophrenic, believed that his writings were simple fact. It's hard to tell what Palmer thought. At one point, he claimed that Shaver's stuff might be "at least 25 percent true."

In the '50s, the two men parted ways. Palmer left *Amazing Stories* to publish *Fate*, which achieved fame by touting the existence of flying saucers. (*Fate* is still publishing and still touting UFOs; *Amazing Stories* lasted in various incarnations until last year.)

Meanwhile, Shaver published his own mag, *Shaver Mystery Magazine*, which appeared only sporadically. Later he claimed he'd discovered detailed written records of Lemuria inside rocks he found on the Wisconsin prairie, but for some reason scientists didn't believe him. In the '60s, the two teamed up again on a magazine called *Hidden World* but it never caught on, possibly because it published Shaver's writings unedited.

America apparently wasn't ready for prose like this: "Life is a scream in the face of a bright madness, then! Life is a silly sound like a death rattle from an insane clown dying in the night, then!"

Both men died in the '70s, and no doubt we'll never see their like again. But in an era when magazines are edited by timid souls who make editorial decisions based on demographic data and focus groups, it's pleasing to recall that at least one editor once achieved success by rewriting the ravings of a madman. ⌐

Shaver's 'Lemuria' revealed by Outre

From News Services

From News Services

Deep in the bowels of the Earth, a mutant race of beings keeps thousands of kidnapped humans as slaves and sex toys before eating them. At least that's what Richard S. Shaver believed and who cares that he was a lunatic? He had a good editor who turned Shaver's screeds into some of the most popular pulp magazine stories of the 1940s.

I'm not making this up. It's too weird to be fiction. The story is recounted in **Outre**, a smart, fun quarterly that is devoted to the history of B-movies, pulp magazines and pinup girls. Bruce Wright's "Fear Down Below: The Curious History of the Shaver Mystery" is the most bizarre nonfiction I've read in years.

The story begins with Raymond A. Palmer, a 4-foot hunchback from Milwaukee who spent his sickly childhood reading science fiction. He published a sci-fi fanzine and in 1938, at age 28, was hired to edit a dying sci-fi mag called **Amazing Stories**.

One day in 1943, one of Palmer's assistants tossed a letter into the wastebasket, muttering about "crackpots." Curious, Palmer picked it out of the trash. It was from Shaver, who wrote that he'd discovered "Mantong," the lost language of Atlantis, which he claimed was the basis of all earthly tongues. Palmer printed the letter and it drew response from readers who said they recognized Mantong phrases in various foreign languages.

When Palmer wrote to Shaver, asking how he'd discovered Mantong, Shaver bombarded Palmer with long, semi-coherent letters, explaining that he'd been working at a Detroit auto plant when his welding gun began suddenly picking up the thoughts of his co-workers. Then the welding gun started broadcasting the sounds of a secret torture session held in a cavern deep in the Earth.

Shaver also sent Palmer a 10,000-word manuscript detailing the secret history of our planet. Thousands of years ago, Earth, then called Lemuria, was occupied by a race of immortal giants, Shaver wrote. But then the sun began emitting poison particles that drove the giants underground, where they mutated into ugly, evil beings called Dero, who kidnap, rape and devour humans.

Your average editor would have tossed Shaver's ravings. Not Palmer. He rewrote the manuscript into a piece called "I Remember Lemuria!," which he billed as fact and published in March 1945. The issue sold out and drew hundreds of letters from readers. For the next four years, Palmer kept rewriting Shaver's fantasies, illustrating them with lurid covers that featured scantily clad women menaced by Dero demons.

Shaver's stories helped boost Amazing Stories' circulation from 27,000 to 185,000. Soon there was a Shaver fan club and monthly fanzine. The **Atlantic Monthly** and **Life** published stories on the phenomenon. Shaver, who was probably a paranoid schizophrenic, believed that his writings were fact.

It's hard to tell what Palmer thought.

In the '50s, the two men parted ways. Palmer left Amazing Stories to publish **Fate**, which touted the existence of flying saucers. (Fate is still publishing and still touting UFOs; Amazing Stories lasted until last year.)

Meanwhile, Shaver published his own mag, **Shaver Mystery Magazine**. Later, he claimed he'd discovered written records of Lemuria inside rocks he found on the Wisconsin prairie. In the '60s, the two teamed up on a magazine called the **Hidden World** but it never caught on, possibly because it published Shaver's writings unedited. America apparently wasn't ready for prose like this: "Life is a silly sound like a death rattle from an insane clown dying in the night, then!"

Both men died in the '70s, and we'll never see their like again. But in an era when magazines are edited by timid souls who make decisions based on focus groups, it's pleasing to recall an editor who achieved success by rewriting the ravings of a madman.

— *Peter Carlson,*
Washington Post

The Sacramento Bee (Sacramento, California)
01 Mar 2001, Thu •Page 42

Even by sci-fi standards, this tale's strange

By Peter Carlson
Washington Post

WASHINGTON – Deep in the bowels of the Earth, a mutant race of malevolent beings keeps thousands of kidnapped humans as slaves and sex toys before ultimately eating them.

At least that's what Richard S. Shaver believed, and who cares that he was a raving lunatic? He had a good editor who turned Shaver's demented screeds into some of the most popular pulp magazine stories of the 1940s.

The whole strange story is recounted in the current issue of Outre magazine, a smart, fun, profusely illustrated quarterly devoted to the history of B-movies, pulp magazines and classic pinup girls.

Outre is six years old, but I'd never seen it until I stumbled upon the latest issue. As I read Bruce Wright's "Fear Down Below: The Curious History of the Shaver Mystery," my jaw dropped and I stood transfixed. It's the most bizarre nonfiction story I've read in years and a delightful look into the hidden history of American magazines.

The story begins with Raymond A. Palmer, a 4-foot-tall hunchback from Milwaukee who spent his sickly childhood reading science fiction.

He founded a sci-fi fan club and published a sci-fi fanzine and in 1938, at age 28, was hired to edit a dying Chicago pulp sci-fi mag called Amazing Stories.

One day in 1943, one of Palmer's assis-

tants tossed a letter from a reader into the
wastebasket, muttering about "crackpots."
Curious, Palmer picked the epistle out of
the trash. It was from Shaver, a then-unknown ex-hobo and construction worker
who wrote that he'd discovered "Mantong,"
the lost language of Atlantis, which he
claimed was the basis of all earthly tongues
Palmer printed the letter and it drew a
considerable response from readers who
said they recognized Mantong phraseology
in various foreign languages.

When Palmer wrote to Shaver, asking
how he'd discovered Mantong, Shaver bombarded the editor with long, semi-coherent
letters, explaining that he'd been working
at a Detroit auto plant when his welding
gun began suddenly picking up the
thoughts of his co-workers.

That was weird enough, but then the
welding gun started broadcasting the
sounds of a secret torture session held in a
cavern deep in the Earth.

Shaver also sent Palmer "A Warning to
Future Man," a 10,000-word manuscript
detailing the secret history of our planet.
Thousands of years ago, Earth, then called
Lemuria, was occupied by a race of immortal giants, Shaver wrote. But then the sun
began emitting poison particles that drove
the giants underground, where they mutated into ugly, evil beings called Dero, who
kidnap and devour humans.

Your average editor would have tossed
Shaver's ravings. Not Palmer.

He rewrote the manuscript into a piece
called "I Remember Lemuria!", which he

billed as fact and published in the March 1945 issue of Amazing Stories.

The issue sold out and drew hundreds of letters from readers. For the next four years, Palmer kept rewriting Shaver's sadistic fantasies, illustrating them with wonderfully lurid covers that featured scantily clad women menaced by Shaver's Dero demons.

"The result," writes Wright, "is an unforgettable blend of high-flying imagination with curiously homely touches, as when we encounter a highly intelligent snail-centaur named Hank." Shaver's stories helped boost Amazing Stories' circulation from 27,000 to 185,000. Soon there was a Shaver cult, complete with a fan club and monthly fanzine. The Atlantic Monthly and Life published stories on the strange phenomenon.

At one point, Palmer claimed that Shaver's stuff might be "at least 25 percent true." In the '50s, the two men parted ways. Palmer left Amazing Stories to publish Fate, which achieved fame by touting the existence of flying saucers. (Fate is still publishing and still touting UFOs; Amazing Stories lasted in various incarnations until last year.) Meanwhile, Shaver published his own mag, Shaver Mystery Magazine, which appeared only sporadically. Later, he claimed he'd discovered detailed written records of Lemuria inside rocks he found on the Wisconsin prairie, but for some reason scientists didn't believe him.

Both men died in the '70s.

Outre is available at full-service newsstands for $5.95 or by subscription for $20 a year at P.O. Box 1900, Evanston, Ill. 60204.

THE ANCIENT ALPHABET
Richard S Shaver

The

HIDDEN WORLD
Spring, 1961

THE ANCIENT ALPHABET

By Richard S. Shaver

Out of the many things I learned from my cavern mentors, one stood out in my mind as truly important: the alphabet of the ancient language they called Mantong. Here was actual proof! Here was a tool that could be used to confirm the ancient race, to trace the remnants existing today, in modern languages. Here was a way to unearth the ancient story of Atlantis, Lemuria (Mu) and the race of Titans and Atlans who inhabited the Earth many thousands of years ago, and who fled the Earth because of a tremendous catastrophe, leaving behind the ancestors of the present-day underground race I called the "dero" and the "tero". Without the alphabet you cannot begin to understand the terminology I will use constantly. Nor, without it, can you check with me in your own way, through actual research of your own that can be done while sitting in your own armchair with results that cannot fail but to astound you.

Although the alphabet is a beginning, and a key, there is also a dictionary; and it is regrettable that such a dictionary cannot be provided in comprehensive form along with the alphabet, for it would be a valuable help, a tremendous shortcut to your rapid understanding of what it is that I am trying to convey to you. Yet, I will append to this exposition of the alphabet a fragmentary dictionary which may be of help in understanding how the language functions. As I progress, your dictionary of the ancient language will increase, and I hope that one of the results of my work will be actual compilation of a complete dictionary.

The alphabet is a strange one, in many respects. First, it is one that causes the etymological experts of philology to snort with disdain, because it violates the time-table they have set up in their so-learned books. Language derivations, they say, go back into ancient times to such languages as Sanskrit, Chinese, Egyptian and Latin and on down to modern times to the so-called Romance languages, Spanish, French, etc. And the most modern of them all is, they say, English, which is largely Anglo-Saxon. The reason for their laughter is my claim that the most ancient of all alphabets, that of Mantong, the one I present to you here, is in English!

"There you are!" they snort. "Obviously the man is wrong. We can prove beyond all possible doubt, even to an idiot, that English is not an ancient language, but is made up of bits of all previous languages, and is a hodge-podge that resulted from just such an amalgamation."

It is here that they have made a serious mistake. Language is phonetic. A sound is a sound, and no matter where uttered, it is the *same* sound. The alphabet is a series of sounds from which words are made. They are the basic building blocks of language. They are called "letters". (Sometimes one wonders why we call them letters, until we think about writing letters (alphabets) and realizing that is how we communicate with each other. Write a letter to your mother once a week, so that she will know how it is with you.) Thus, the Mantong alphabet is presented in the only way in which it can be presented, as *sounds*. The only way I have to present these sounds is in their English equivalent. Yet, I do not try to evade the philologists by so meek a tactic—I say here and now, beyond all possible revocation, that English is *closer* to the original language of Man than any other language; and it is closer because it is not an amalgamation, but the mother lode of all language.

There are many meanings attached to the letters. For instance, Churchward has the alphabet telling the story of the sinking of ancient Mu; each letter in order, being a portion of that tale. This is easy to do, by simply ascribing the proper meaning to each letter. Yet all these things, on which I advance no opinion one way or the other, are evidence that it is a popular concept that the individual letters do have meanings. But what are those meanings, *actually?*

What other meanings could they have than those useful in compiling words that describe what it is wished that they describe?

Sometimes to make a point, we must first make an assumption. Here I will make one, but actually it is putting the cart before the horse, because if I waited until I had introduced the horse, I would follow naturally with the cart. Our horse is the assumption that this ancient race did exist. It did, but I haven't described it to you as yet except in fiction—so if you will bear with me, I will speak as though you were already convinced of the reality of that ancient race which I have (I believe) actually contacted.

This ancient race is not native to Earth. It comes from Space, and it is ancient beyond belief in the sense that it is hundreds of millions of years old, and Earth is but a baby in comparison, the race actually pre-dating the formation of the planet itself. One of the things done by the ancient race is the "seeding down" of new planets to humanity. Obviously my readers will see that I am going contrary to the ordinary concept of evolution, since what I am saying is that Man did not evolve on this planet, but was placed here, just as he has been placed on many other planets, some of them long dissolved and gone into the primal elements from which they were originally created. Yet I do not say that evolution does not happen, from the original cell implanted in the primal ocean to the complex animal forms that walk the land and fly through the air. Man is none of these.

Picture, if you will, Man placed on a young planet, teeming with evolved life. He is placed there to master it (and himself). One of his first needs is communication. Those who placed him there have a language, a basic one, which if reason is used, is obviously always the same basic pattern. It is a collection of sounds which it is possible for the human voice to reproduce. Now, if those sounds were meaningless in themselves, they would contain no meaning even when collected in groups. If "A" has no meaning nor "P", nor "E", then neither has APE. So, A, P, and E have individual meanings. Put together they have a meaning that *perfectly* describes an APE. If one member of this ancient race I am speaking of were to meet another member on a far planet from Earth, and were to describe the evolved life forms of Earth, he could get across to his hearer a perfect picture of what an Earth Ape is, simply by the word which describes it. No picture would be necessary. If the letters in the word have a definite meaning, the word meaning should be quite clear to the person having a complete knowledge of the basic meanings of the letters.

Thus, as we read in the Bible: "And out of the ground the Lord God formed every beast of the field and every fowl of the air; and brought them unto Adam to see what he would call them: and whatsoever Adam called every living creature, that was the name thereof. And Adam gave names to all cattle, and to the fowl of the air, and to every beast of the field . . ." (Genesis 2:19, 20) You will note that even the Bible agrees that the beasts and fowl were formed out of the ground, or by evolutionary processes, but that man was formed differently: "And the Lord God formed man of the dust of the ground, and breathed into his nostrils the breath of life and man became a living soul." (Genesis 2:7) Note that he was formed out of the "dust" of the ground. This "dust" is the same I will describe to you later as "exd". Adam was compete, when formed, with no intermediate forms. He did not come "out of the ground". He then received the "breath of life" and became a "living soul" right then and there. Later on, when we study the words with the meaning of the alphabet before us, we will get a very exciting picture out of the Book of Genesis.

The point I want to make here is the "naming" of the animals, etc., by Adam. Adam, you won't argue was the "first man". Reasonably he cannot be anything else but a member of the ancient race, of the "first men". Not an animal. Not an evolutionary product of the planet Earth. Adam named all of the animals *correctly,* and the key he used in naming them was the alphabet. He knew what each letter meant, and when he saw the animal, brought before him by the Lord God, he inspected it, and pieced together the proper letters into a word that would describe the animal, so that the uttering of the word would identify the animal, even though not seen by the hearer of the word. This is very important and should be perfectly obvious. If a language is a method of communication, it must be exactly that, and not a meaningless symbolism which must be accompanied in all cases with a sample of the item being spoken of. We cannot carry an elephant with us to show our hearer what we mean by the word. It is not a matter of association. Such a language would be quite impractical, and once the object were non-existent, the word would be meaningless. I will admit that much of our own language today is meaningless. We teach the meanings of words strictly by association. It is a matter of memory, solely. A visitor from another world, hearing our spoken words, could not possibly know what we were talking about.

But with the meanings of the sounds (the letters) clear in his mind, he could dissect our words, and discover our basic meaning. He could communicate with us, with *any* race, without the process of a complete memorization (and association with his own language) of our language done laboriously by uttering the word, and showing him simultaneously the object the word is supposed to represent. He could not identify an Ape-word without the Ape-object beside it. Thereafter he would remember it—and how confused he would be to hear the word "ape" later on and be told it didn't mean an animal at all, but the act of imitation.

There *is* a basic universal meaning to every sound (and therefore to every written letter representing that sound—and the writing of the letter also comes from a pictorial source, pictography).

When you want to name something, you form a word. Then you tack that word onto the object, and associate the two, and memorize the association. You "coin" a word. You use letters in making it up. You also use two or more words in combination. The result is meaningless to everybody but ourselves until we "educate" them to the meaning; *unless* we use the true meaning of the letters. Many of our words today, in the English language, and in any other language for that matter, are basically meaningless, and also present a totally false meaning, because they are just happenstance combinations of letters chosen at random to "tag" a new object or idea or action.

But when Adam named the animals, he was using the basic, unchanging meanings of the sounds (letter), and he named correctly. What is unfortunate it that the phonetics have come down to us either distorted or lost in many cases, and we find the words paradoxical, even when viewed from the Alphabet base. When Adam said "Ape", just how did it *sound?* Say it out loud. Ape. *Two* sounds! *Not* three! A broad A and an explosive "P". The *proper* phonetic spelling of Ape is "Ap." When Adam said it, did he say: "A-pe?" I think he did. Today we have lost the phonetics in part, retaining only the written form which includes the "E". Why the "E"? Because without it, the word Ape does not mean the animal Adam named! What impressed Adam was the likeness of the ape to man with the added factor he did not possess, the *great power* of the ape! An ape was a creature similar to himself but with great power, enormous energy.

By now you must have grasped the meaning of at least one of the letters of the ancient alphabet. P means *power.* Whenever Adam saw an animal whose power impressed him, he *quite logically,* and *by necessity,* included the letter "P" in the word that described that animal.

Now you will want to know what "E" means, and why Adam placed that letter *after* the "P" in Ape? When one letter modifies or compliments another, it is placed immediately following it. E is *energy.* It is an overall concept of energy, and includes the idea of motion. The only way the ape could express his power was through motion, yet the power was there even when he did not move. He possessed the energy and it need not be applied to him from some outside source. When he wanted to use his power, he simply went into action, into movement. He was: Animal with Powerful Energy. And there you have the meaning of "A". It is "animal"; and the word was used more correctly as "An."

Now, before I go any further, I will give you the alphabet, with meanings, so that you may follow me in a few simple expositions of the use of the alphabet. From there you can proceed on your own—you will have the vital tool necessary to proceed. And the results cannot fail to astonish you.

THE MANTONG ALPHABET

A— Animal (used AN for short.)

B— Be. To exist (Often used as a "command".)

C— Con. To See (C-on: to understand.)

D— De. Detrimental, disintegant energy. (The second most important symbol in the alphabet.)

E— Energy. (An all-pervading concept including the idea of motion.)

F— Fecund. (Used "fe", as in fe-male—fecund man.)

G— Generate. (Used "gen".)

H— Human. (A very metaphysical concept here, not fully understood, but used in the sense "H-you-man": a human is an H-man.)

I— Self. Ego. (Same as our English I.)

J— Generate (A duplication of G, but with a delicate difference in shade of meaning. Actually Je, in contrast to Ge is a very important distinction. G is the generating energy while J is animal generation per se.)

K— Kinetic. (The force of motion.)

L— Life.

M— Man.

N— Seed. Sport. (Child, as "ninny".)

O— Orifice. (A source concept.)

P— Power.

Q— Quest. (As "quest-ion".)

R— Horror. Danger. (Used AR; symbol of a dangerous quantity of disintegrant force in the object.)

S— Sun. (Used "sis"; an important symbol, always referring to a "sun" whose energy is given off through atomic disintegration.)

T— Integration. Growth. (Used TE; the most important symbol of the alphabet; the true origin of the cross symbol. It signifies the integrative force of growth; as, all matter is growing —the intake of gravity is the cause. The force is T. TIC means the science of growth. Integration-I-see (understand).

U— You.

V— Vital. (Used as VI; the stuff Mesmer called "animal magnetism").

W— Will.

X— Conflict. (Force lines crossing each other.)

Y— Why.

Z— Zero. Nothing. Neutralization. (A quantity of energy of T neutralized by an equal quantity of D. Futility.)

In presenting this alphabet to you, I have given you, in my estimation, one of the most valuable pieces of information you will ever receive in this life. It is inestimably useful, and thorough, thoughtful study of it will reveal that fact to you. It is immensely important, but to understand takes a good head, as the alphabet will reveal in language a rather strange sort of multiple-thought (like many "puns" on the subject). Many times you will believe the result is meaningless, unless you bear in mind the subtle "under-thought" that always seems to be present, often of a very humorous nature.

As an example, let us take the word "trocadero". You have no doubt often seen it used as the name for a nightclub, or a theatre, or any place where entertainment is offered. In applying the alphabet to the word, we come up with this: T-Ro-See-A-D-Ro. (Tero see a dero.) Ro is an ancient word, first one you'll include in your dictionary of the ancient language of Atlan, meaning "controlled"; patterned by a governing force from an AR source, a "horrible" source. (Matter is horrible, in another of those delicate shades of meaning that will be fully explained by me later in my description of the ancient race's science.) The meaning of trocadero, said simply is: Good one see a bad one. So, originally the word trocadero was coined to describe the very bad plays that were perpetrated in the name of entertainment. Today we have forgotten the "pun" intended, the derisive application of the word to the calibre of actors and plays given in the period of the origin of the word, and we apply it only to the *place* where such plays are given. So next time you go to "The Trocadero", don't be surprised if you aren't overly enthusiastic about the quality of the entertainment being offered. Instead, have a good laugh at the owner who so aptly named his establishment!

Let us take the word "romantic." Today it has a meaning largely referring to being sentimental about love. This is a far cry from the meaning we get when we study the word with the alphabet. RO-MAN-TIC (to break it down into the three ancient words of which it is composed) means "the science by which man is controlled" Man is ro to this science. To break it down into individual letters; Horror-source- man-animal- integration-I-see. The horrible source of the man-animal's integration is understood by me. I know how to control man's growth. I am *romantic!* It is very interesting to note that in the late 18th century and early 19th century, a movement of art and literature that subordinated form and finish to content, intellect to emotion, reason to imagination and intuition, the critical to the creative, cleverness and wit to tenderness and pathos, and which emphasized the mystery and beauty of life; typified in France by Rousseau, in Germany by Goethe, Schelling, Schlegel, Lessing, etc., in England by Gray, Cowper, Burns, Coleridge, Wordsworth, Southey, Byron, Shelley, Keats, Rossetti and Carlyle, was called *Romanticism!* The word still has that connotation today, and many others. The romantic era was a period of man's growth in mentality, character and more tender, worthwhile things.

When the arrow was invented, it had to be named. It was aptly named! It was *doubly* horrible, hence the two R's. It "controlled" animals (and man-animals) quite effectively!

A mechanic is a man-animal who understands mech (machines). Mech is another word for your ancient dictionary. MEK. Man's Kinetic Energy made usable. By means of the kinetic energy in metals (and other substances as well) man was able to perform work. He invented a way to use the energy kinetic in matter to accomplish things. A machine's metals moved and therefore performed work, gave off energy.

Not so many years ago a clever man invented a toy which he called "mechano". It was a toy composed of pieces of fabricated metal, nuts and bolts, wheels, string, gears and cogs, a small hand-crank, or even a tiny electric motor. It was called a very constructive, educational toy. It was named mechano. It is amazing to think that the word, supposedly not an ancient word at all, but brand new, coined in modern times, breaks down so aptly in the ancient alpha-

the tree, of which I commanded thee, saying, Thou shalt not eat of it: cursed is the ground for thy sake; in sorrow shalt thou eat of it all the days of thy life; Thorns also and thistles shall it bring forth to thee; and thou shalt eat the herb of the field; In the sweat of thy face shalt thou eat bread, till thou return unto the ground; for out of it wast thou taken: for dust thou art, and unto dust shalt thou return. And Adam called his wife's name Eve; because she was the mother of all the living. Unto Adam also and to his wife did the Lord God make coats of skins, and clothed them. And the Lord God said, Behold the man is become as one of us, to know good and evil: and now, lest he put forth his hand, and take also of the tree of life, and eat, and live forever: Therefore the Lord God sent him forth from the Garden of Eden, to till the ground from whence he was taken." (Genesis 3-17:23.)

When we read these verses of the Bible, we are confused. It seems that before the breaking of the commandment not to eat of the tree, Adam did not eat herbs, nor bread. Was it because it was not necessary while in the Garden? And when the Lord God "clothed" Adam and Eve in skins, wasn't this unnecessary, for did not the Lord God find the pair hiding in the garden, already wearing clothes to hide their nakedness? And does not the Lord God speak very mysteriously when he says "the man is becoming one of us"? Adam is cursed back to the dust from whence he came, but specifically to the *ground,* in which we have already noted a distinction from dust? It is hard to understand.

Until we look at the word BAN in the light of the alphabet, Adam was commanded to *be an animal!* Now it all becomes logical. Adam did not eat herbs and bread before his fall, because he wasn't an animal. Was it because he was a spirit, like the Lord God and his mysterious companions, to whom he speaks? When the Lord God clothed Adam and Eve in skins, when they already had made their own clothing, was it rather in *flesh* that he clothed them? When he sentenced them to the ground, was it to the Earth!

Remember the angel with the flaming sword placed "to the east of Eden" to prevent Adam from returning to the garden? What was to prevent him from re-entering on the west?

In ancient times, the four "cardinal" points of the compass were East-West-North-South, just as they are today; with two distinctions. The Earth was pictured as a flat disk, divided in half by a line. The hemisphere on one side was called North, the hemisphere on the

bet, the ancient dictionary. Mech (by which) animal-man knows, or learns. An instructive mechanical toy. Yet we can all look up the ancient Mechanistic cult of thousands of years ago, to find the word is not new.

One of the most surprising uses to which you can put the alphabet, and one that offers a test of its authenticity, because results are far beyond the possibility of chance, is its use in determining the meaning of words in other languages than English, languages you do not understand. These words should first be taken in their phonetic spelling, and sometimes can be further translated by their actual written form.

Have someone speak foreign words to you that you do not already know. Apply the meanings of this alphabet to the phonetics, and then tell what you think the word means. In the Romance languages, the percentage of "hits" will be low, but still far beyond chance, while the more ancient the language the higher the ability to decipher the meaning.

As a rather random thought (and you will discover many little things such as the following in your search through words with the alphabet), the English word is God, which figures out: Generate-Source-Detrimental. Obviously this should prove the alphabet to be wrong in a very important way, because God certainly does not generate from a detrimental source! However, when we consider the German word Gott, we have occasion to think rather deeply. In German, Gott generates (or creates) from an *integrative* source and further the integation is so important that it is repeated. There are two Ts. Super-integration. Not just forming already existing materials into objects, but forming the very material itself!

In connection with the letter B, the word BAN is closely associated in the sense that B is a command. Be an animal, is what the word ban tells us. But here we are puzzled again. Apparently this is not true. When we tell something to be an animal, we do not ban it! That is a contradiction. Ban is a word that means to forbid, in our present dictionary. It means "stay away to exist". Generally, if one is banned, or banished, he must stay away, for to return is punishable by death. To banish is to put out, put away. Once more we refer to our Bible.

The command here, is Be Animal. When Adam and Eve were banished from the Garden of Eden, the Lord God said: "Because thou hast hearkened unto the voice of thy wife, and hast eaten of

other, South. East was *down* and West was *straight up*. This mythological belief has always been ignored by the learned, but it did exist. In the light of the alphabet's meaning of the word BAN, and the flaming sword only on one side of the garden it becomes quite logical. Adam and Eve were cast from the Garden of Eden, which does not exist on the surface of the Earth (is that why it cannot be found!), to the *east*. The only way back to it was in a westward or *upward* direction! Is there any confirmation of this? Yes! In the Lost Books of the Bible, in the book of Adam and Eve, it tells of Adam's many trips to the top of the highest mountain, where he stared longingly up into Eden (still 18 cubits out of reach) to which he so wished to return. Today when we die we still "go west"!

Try reading Genesis through, applying the alphabet to all the words used, and prepare for many surprises. No matter how you use the alphabet, an intelligent application of it will immerse you in the most astounding revelations, and induce the most incredible brand of thinking and you may well find the subject so enormous that it overcomes you.

I regret that simply giving the alphabet as I have here does not provide half enough information to render this magnificent tool truly effective. For instance, you must understand more fully the science behind the two letters T and D.

The Devil, the protagonist of the D-evil. Dis, the de that happens to the ego because of the sun. Tic, the science of growth. Vi, the energy of sex. Ar, the thing that makes a spirit shun the sun, the secret behind the reason we believe ghosts appear at night.

Fe, the female man! Refer to the passages quoted from the Bible in the foregoing, and note that Adam *did not name his wife* until *after* he had been banned! Then he named her Eve. Fe. The vital energy of sex. The *mother* of all the *living*.

Communication! A language that is not just a memorized jingle, a vulnerable set of symbols whose meaning can be lost in a flood, or a fire, or an exploding planet. The Alphabet of the Angels! The English alphabet! The alphabet of the Angles!

A DICTIONARY OF THE MANTONG LANGUAGE

Richard S Shaver

The

HIDDEN WORLD

Spring, 1961

A DICTIONARY OF THE MANTONG LANGUAGE

By Richard S. Shaver

Anti. Now means against anything. Then the meaning was much the same, but subtly different. Literally: "animal tie". But "tie" to them means same as it does in "time". Time is a word which is obvious - tie me, says time, and of course one can't; so it is a picturesque name for it. Anti is a similar word meaning one who blocks a proposed plan by holding to the present one. "An" seems to have meant life unit—it was "an" instead of man, for many of them were not men at all, but very different from men in form.

Alone. Animal with low attraction for other animals; a - animal, lo—low and ne—name for the magnetic force of attraction between animals. Ne is a root word used for complementary force activity.

Amass. Animal gathers things together into a mass; a - animal and mass - (the same) mass.

Aqua. Water - meant literally, "I am the thing you look for most". a—an, q—quest, u—you, and a—an. An quests you an. Why the extra a I don't know, but it is derived from a tongue alien to English has been through another tongue.

Abode. An be o de. Fully: "Here is one who wills to exist, oh thou who wills death". A—the same, be—to exist, O—same, etc. Probably a sign over a door like our NO TRAMPS.

Absent An be sent, "one was sent".

Absurd. An be surd - s err d, or s you d. One has erred from sun destructive, same as our "crazy with the heat".

Accost. An see one who co's t. Was same as our "Gillette me have a nickel for a cup of coffee". Said in one word, it means: "See, I am one who cooperates to build a good social pattern". Was probably used to open conversations by those who wished to sell or beg.

Acid. An see I de. A label still used and a very obvious one derived intact from the antique language. Literally: POISON.

Accident. An see dent - or, an see, I have experienced a blow. Dent was much used: o de always means a decrease, a hollow spot, a depression, anything "less".

Accretion. A-c-re-t-ion. An see rebuilding the growth. This one is obvious, needs little explanation. Tion was used a great deal, meant any healthy unit of any kind.

Acme. Highest point was expressed by saying - you will see me. Animal see me.

Acorn. An see ore seed. A—an, c—see, or—ore and n—seed. Useful seed.

Acrobat. A—an, c—see, ro—robot. Bat be a t. Bat, as in combat, means active life. May also be thus: a ball bat—thus a combat is COME-BAT and a robat a juggler of bats (as Indian clubs). This is rather an obvious one. The "act" of a robat.

Acrid. A—an, c—see, ri—wry and d—detrimental. See, I am a wry substance. Note and remember the used roots such as ri and bat and ro are the language.

Access. An see opening. This is rather a difficult one to explain without getting "suggestive", for they did not have our repugnance to sex and being plain about what they meant. Ess always seems to have meant what we mean when we say "a nice ass", etc. It is still the feminine ending in French as Modess, actress etc. Thus "an accessible woman" came to mean anything accessible. What is usually difficult is here accessible is what the word means. It often seems that our vulgar speech is richer in the old clean root words than our formal talk, that they survived without foreign, ununderstandable admixtures of roots twisted through another way of using the tongue. Thus Brooklynese" and "Backwoods" talk intermingled are hard to understand, especially how they got that way.

Acute. An see you attract. T or te always means attract or grow or both. Te is actually always an attractive force in action and de is always a repellant force in action. "One approves his thought".

Adder. A der. The animal is a der. Just as the bottle is labeled acid, so is the deadly animal labeled.

Advent. Literally: "Made another opening". Ad is often used to indicate add. Vent was used as today, too, and the use of de would indicate the opening was downward. Thus an advent is made by descending a stair through a crowd.

Adventure. Here vent means wound. To adventure means to add to your wounds. The re on the end means it turns out all right, if adventure. If it was add wounds and die, it would be adventured. These subtle meanings have been lost and another system of meaning grafted on, thus de means past. It meant past then, too, but in a different sense.

Apparent. As through a rent. Par has quite a meaning and is used often. Here par gives the sense of a wide rent, easily seen through.

Arrant. Ar always meant "bad by sound" - a dangerous sound. Arrant seems to mean one who makes a lot of frightening noise. An ar ant - an ant always does the same thing over and over, thus an arr ant is a person who always makes a dangerous sound. An err ant is one who always errs, and pedant one who always figures out a dire conclusion, etc.

Arrest. Animal stops to rest. The ar syllable means is dangerously stopped. You always get a rest when arrested.

Atlantean. ATLANTEAN IS ONE OF MY STAR WITNESS-ES. It means in Webster - gigantic, huge. If you read my stories you will know why it means huge without more explanation.

Attraction. One is drawn on the track of t ions - tions are always drawn inward - one is drawn toward the object - track t.

August. Aug for augmentation and gust for a flow of energy. Thus an august person is one who makes you feel important too, just meeting him, because of the augmenting vitality that comes to you from him. An augmentative gust. Aug and mag seem to mean the same thing, but are different. Aug means augment and mag magnify which are very different in truth. Aug—strengthen and mag— make larger. These are root words and should be remembered.

Attain. Ain seems to have meant "own". Attain would mean: this healthy an acquires ownership. Our ain't is not a contraction of are and not but was a word meaning hands off, it's mine. It ain't yours, I own it, you don't. Its use has corrupted.

Automatic. Self acting - note aug and mag and aut and mat. Man is in truth an automatic electrical mechanism. Automatic meant self mating - aut self plus aug and mat - self growing and self mating meant entirely self contained. I don't think the men of the middle ages invented any of these words or made them up out of Latin roots, but found most of them in use on manuscripts since lost. Our Latin students of the Middle Ages made up a lot of confusing explanations which cost us the true origin of our language. The Latin and Greek had the same or nearly the same origin, but our words in very few cases came from the Latin or Greek, but were thought to by the so called students of the middle ages who had in fact, infinitely fewer books than a student of Alexandria in 200 BC. It was his very poor work, that religious student of Medieval times, which has lost us our immense heritage of wisdom from the ancient God race. None of them dared even think of Paganism, and Pagans were the God race who were infinitely beyond even modern men in science. So anything of the kind was destroyed, and all writing was in Christian hands, who dared not even harbor an ancient book of truth for fear of burning as a witch. Such books did exist, and some men could read them, but dared not admit it publicly for fear of death as a witch or sorcerer. So those dark centuries cost us all the true knowledge left us by the great past. Those were the books still spoken of as The Books of Magic. They *were* magic, for they were better science than we possess today.

Arid. Same as dry. A wry d, and a d wry are the same.

Axe. X is always the conflict sign. Two forces cross and clash. X marks the spot. An axe is any weapon for the purpose.

Balderdash. To be all *detrimental* err, and to dash off a lot of it. What I think of most writing, by other writers.

Beauteous. Be you te us. You attract us.

Beget. To cause to exist. Be—to exist, g for generate.

Beguile. To cause ill to exist.

Being. To be in generation. A fecund person. A being is one able to beget.

Bend. To cause to bow down. De is often plain *down*.

Bewail. To be in the way of ill. A sound indicating ill fate. Be way ill.

Blockade. To block a de. De is often short for dero.

Bode. To prophesy disaster (note dis astir). "Be, oh de".

Brain. An important word, indicating they knew the cells of the brain use a ray to communicate with each other (though ray seems to have meant any continuation - seems to have been used to indicate a family line, any flow etc.) In this case, the *ra* is the intent to continue to exist - a be ray, and *in* means all life inside. Same as micro life - IN seems to indicate small individuals here. *In* is a basic word, often used.

Bride. You figure this out, the censor won't let me. Be ride. Be wry de.

Bright. The smart are apt to be right.

Bald. De is here used in its below zero sense. As te is a quantity of be force, z is none at all and de is negative, less than nothing. So, to be all de - to have less than no hair. Probably originated as a joke, meaning: "He has so much de in his head, it burnt all his hair off".

Bad. Be a de. To be a negative destructive force - a character dominated by the *delusory* flows of disintegrance instead of thought flows.

Bandit. Be the an de I te. Literally, "if an animal is destructive I join him to my band." They seem to have used *an* instead of *man* a great deal, principally because many members of society were not in truth *men,* but they *were* all animals. They were a hybrid race from space, of many shapes. There was perhaps no standard shape, the criterion of race being grade of intelligence rather than two arms, two legs and a human head. The te always means - to bind to one, to tie. As a magnet - a binding net of attraction.

Bard. One who bars out de - as in lady, who allays the depressing de force. Lady and bard were complimentary terms, meaning you overjoy us, you decrease our depression.

Barred. Note same use - de is barred out.

Base. Be an s e. This animal is ruled by sun energy.

Belt. Be - l - t. Life binding. In the act - as in belie - in the act of lying, etc.

Big. In the act of generation - as pregnant. In truth same word as pregnant. Be I generate. Here bi is also two - is often used as two, as in bigamy, etc.

Bilin. Here note the use of *in* to indicate dissolved matter, or material of small size, found in bile. Be ill in. In is an important word.

Bilk. Be ill kinetic. K—movement, ill - not wise. To run away unwisely - to escape from just due - to dodge.

Birth. Note bi, of two. Rt is a contraction of right. H—human. Thus - of two right humans is one of good birth.

Bit. Cutting blade - a drill etc. Be I te. T - strongly integrative. A tough tool.

Bitt. Same - place where cables are fastened - tough metal.

Blab. If lady is one who allays de, then blab is to allay be. To decrease the chance of being. Thus a blabber is one who makes it unsafe by talk.

Blind. Be life within de. De in its sense as less than nothing. Life in de - a dismal place to be - to deprive of light.

Blink. A glimpse on the run (k). A tiny fleeting light. A tiny glimpse of life on the run.

Blob. Be low be. A bubble - a blister - an amoeba is a blob. Also means not very dense, fragile, a little jelly.

Bodice. Be less so I see. "Oh top of dress, be less". I can see more.

The bodice, or place we like low, in a dress.

Cap. Geo. Crile says electric to run the body is made in the brain - or mostly held in brain. Thus cap is - see animal power.

Circle. C—see, ir—err, c—see, le—life energy. Sample of their warning words. When you err mentally, you direct life energy in such a way that nothing is accomplished of true self interest. You arrive where you started. Most of us are no better off at the end of a day than when we began the day, in fact worse off, for we have spent all our available body energy to no real result. Thus most of us are in err, we get nowhere, and our children repeat the routine circle - useless effort to the grave again. The energy must be directed wholly at the point of self interest - and this is never oppositional to other interests for that is cancellation. All efforts must be coincidental directional efforts toward attaining more energy, stronger life. Or we circle.

Cogent. Co gen te. One who cooperates in the generation of a strong fabric of government.

Cereal. See re all. To re is to rebuild. Food for all.

Cite. See I te. To quote - to recommend - a citation.

Code. See Oh de. A warning label for lawbreakers. Code meant see, what happens when you de. "Oh de".

Con. An important root word. Con—See on. Conning tower, conscience - all such words are derivative. To see ahead.

Concise. To see ahead and cut off briefly. To cut in the right place is to be concise when speaking.

Condor. Nice descriptive word. To con de or. The condor flies very high looking for the product of detrimental, death.

Conquer. Look ahead on the quest of err. To conquer is exactly what Hitler has done - looked ahead long to end up in the greatest disaster for all. Thus was a conqueror understood by them. And so he is today. There are a great many con words and you will learn a lot of the antique language figuring them out.

Create. See re a te. To make again something - so create seems to have meant to remake. Nothing can be created wholly, its parts must exist in energy, but that all possible combinations have occurred before must have been their thought.

Cruel. See rue life. When you see cruel, you see something to make you rue life.

Crypt. Crypt means "underground room" and cryptology means "sacred language". Where else would the Gods' language exist than in crypts since they lived in caves to avoid the sun? And that is just the meanings given for these words. Why the connection between crypt and language - between underground room and writing? Because for centuries, the only writing on earth existed in the ancient uninhabited sacred caves, the homes of the gods.

Cub. See you be. Baby, too, is a word—be a be why. Grow, baby grow, but is there a reason? Meaning you're pretty dumb yet, you annoy me. *Babe* is the well behaved baby.

Dandy. De an de why. A terribly dangerous little animal, he looks. Just why dandy should mean dressed I don't know, unless they mean a useless attempt at prettifying a horrible person by use of clothes. Thus a dandy would mean a dressed up ruffian.

Dark. Ar seems to be best illustrated by the word horror and the harrow. Thus dark is harrowing detrimental movement from the things we are apt to see in the dark.

Death. De an te h. The te force of the human obliterated by disintegrant energy (de).

Debit. De bit. Bit by detrimental. Less. A hole in my credit.

Decease. Stopped by de.

Decent. An important word, still used as stage slang. They call at the dressing room door to see if you are decent. Not in a condition embarrassing to self. "The de has been sent from my body".

Decide. I see the de and I de the de. I decide what to do about the detrimental aspects of a situation.

Decumbent. De come bent. De has lain me down. Bent to earth by the coming of de.

Defeat. Overcome by de.

Defile. A slot (in a mountain). A notch (de) as if cut by a file.

Deform. Form distorted by de.

Deicide. Now means God murder. Then - I side with de.

Desolate. De sol ate. The sun detrimental ate everything. A burned place.

Deviate. De vi ate. The de has eaten the vital force. Implication being that the thing or man errs in direction because of subjection to destructive force.

Devil. De vile. To be vile with de. A person whose body is heavily infected with detrimental disintegrance, so as to cause completely destructive tendencies.

Discharge. Dis is always repellant. Dis is short for disintegrant energy. To be discharged is to be sent out.

Disillusion. The disillusion is an important concept as it effects much prominent thought today. The disillusion is a mental slant that says nothing is possible. One is disillusioned when one learns that men ignorantly harbor this illusion without knowing it is not true thought.

Discompose. Dis come pose. If dis did come and pose we would have disorder in front of us.

Dissolution. Dis solut ion. A solution of dis, in the process decomposing one's body, is dissolute. The body fluids contain more dis force than te force.

Down. De own. To be owned by is to be down. To go down is to succumb to de.

Droll. De roll. To fall down - and roll like a fool - is droll. Most sure laugh getter of most comedians is the fall.

Drop. De ro p. De controls power, therefore it falls.

Drunk. De run kinetic. Run about destructively.

Erode.. E ro de. Energy ro's to de. Corrosion of anything.

Errant. Err ant. To wander like an ant, in err directions.

Erratic. Err a tic. Tic is the word for life science of government economy. To err tic is to fail to understand what to do to keep things "ticking".

Evolution. Vol is a much used basic, as in INVOLUNTARY - the in vol rules. The will of the cells. In evolution it means the will of energy (the surrounding field of determining factors of energy flow which makes life what it is). Literally: The will of energy forms the life ions.

Fecund. Fe cund. One of those "earthy" words.

Female. Fe male. Simply, fecund male.

Ferocious. Fe ro see us. A robot to the impulse of hunger sees us. Hunger as in sex or food.

Fusion. F u s ion. Fecund sun ion (melting).

Fusil. The same, with a detrimental connotation.

Future. Fecund t will bring you the power of rebuilding. You will continue to exist. Future—what continues to exist.

Gad. G a d. To generate a detrimental. The point of a spear. Note goad - the same. To make a hole - gad.

Galleon. Here the use of all is typical - to generate a le which is all embracing. So big it makes all lee. In alligator note all - the all gate. Gate is often used for mouth.

Garter. Gar ter. Ter means to hold too tightly - or frozen - to err in inward attraction. Gar is to generate har (as in harrow). Thus a garter is a harrowing device to hold things tightly.

Glad. Lad is same as in lady - to be glad is to generate inwardly a force which allays de force.

Goddess. Here the frank use of ess is evident as female indication.

Grot. Means cave. A cave is excluding de by rock insulation, hence a grot is a place that gens ro te, or good men.

Harakira. A Japanese word indicating same roots in their language. Har - a - kir - a. We know har as in harrow. Kir is too fast. Thus one commits harakira, because the harrowing experiences occur too rapidly to allow one to wish to live longer. The k also indicates the impact of a rapidly moving thing when followed by ir. The Japs learned that for every action or motion in energy there is an equal and opposite reaction. They dropped bombs - bombs come back.

Hauteur. High err. Hyba is an Indian word meaning top of anything; haut in French is height in English. The height of err is hauteur.

Helot. He lo t. Slave. One without attraction or standing in the government - which seems often to have been meant by t. The t of a country - that which holds it together, as well as its value to one. Lo te would be one didn't get much out of things.

Harem. Why it's harrowing to be in harem you will have to figure out. Probably something about supply and demand.

Hellibore. A plant - with long roots - a dangerous drug.

Helve. Hel ve. Hell's vital energy is all I get for axe handle.

Hero. He ro. One who ro's to masculine energy - literally "all man".

Hostess. Their social life was very different from ours!

Hostile. The host is different here; he doesn't like you. Of course, he is ill, or he wouldn't be that way.

Hose. Ho see. What we say in other words at hose on some legs. Also another of those down-to-earth words.

Hospital. Ho spital. Place where everybody spits. Latter day word when there was lots of tb. It *didn't* come from the Latin or Greek *hospiceaa.*

Hotel. Ho tel. "Ho, come and talk". Place where everything is told.

Huge. Much the same word as big. You gen human. A great growth.

Iciness. Ic in ess. State of being icy. Extremely cold. An expressive word—they were very salty and alive.

Illapse. Ill lapse. Gradual sliding.

Immoral. Im mor al. Always trying to make more of something.

Immortal. The same, only they live longer.

Impetus. Meaning of im is vague, but p t us is power good for us.

Inactive. Active only inwardly. Living but unmoving. It doesn't derive from the *inaecea,* meaning disease, but from English words in and act.

Indent. In a dent. (Dent - de inward.)

Ingrain. In g ra in. Inwardly genning rays in - as lines in a tree trunk are rays from center etc.

Inn. The n means seed. Was it a bawdy house?

Insane. In s an. Animal is a sun robot. Note mad - may de. Inwardly burning. In s.

Intelligence. In tel I gen, see. My *in* tells me things. A thinker.

Interlace. In ter lay ce. To lay between in a way that holds (t) tightly.

Interrogate. In ter ro gate. One who has too much the interest of the government at heart. Makes his mouth go—rogate, (note as in alligator). A robot to mouthiness asks too many questions.

Ionic. Ion seems to have been used for any charged chamber, as in mansion - man's home. That their homes were charged with beneficial electric is rather sure. Ion is still a charged particle. Ic is science - thus ionic is science or building homes. Wonder what doric houses were like?

Isolate. Note use of sol to indicate division - I sol ate. Disintegrance divides things - always. To isolate. To set apart.

Issue. Note iss - for offspring. Come forth. Note (Isis). Why ess and iss should be the same you should see.

J. J and G were the same letter which acquired a different form from different races forming the letter differently.

Jilt. J il t is to gen ill t. To get mad at and leave.

Jut. Gen you. Te to stick out strongly.

Kitten. N for seed, k for run. A little thing that runs about.

Know. Now is time to move - to know when.

Laconic. La con ic. One who understands life science; therefore can be "matter of fact".

Lady. To lay de. Allay depression. Complimentary term.

Lair. Where lies a life undependable. A wild beast lays here.

Lain. To lay in.

Lass. Just what it says.

Laundry. Lawn and dry, dried on the lawn.

Lewd. Life will de. One with a de will.

Lineage. The age line. The line through the ages.

Lice. Look before you lie down. Lie and see. You will learn later.

License. Lie and sense. This sense is the same root as censor. One lies with the permission of the censor. Strange customs, they had.

Legal. This is a very complicated meaning from lee and all. *All* meaning *state* which generates a *lee* of safety for the individual who is *legal.* It is a significant word illustrating their usage of these basic words.

Legate. An ambassador who shares this lee, though not of the state. The gate means he can go in and out of state without hindrance - has a lee gate of safety.

Legend. Any imperishable legend—rather writing—as title of a book or immortal words. The de of time is on the end, meaning to gen a lee against de - to become immortal by writings which do not perish. (Lee—same sense as lee of a boat.)

Leader. One who forms a lee against der. A thinker who can be relied on to detect detrimental err in plans.

Levity and *levitate.* To leave it - to float. The former mentally the latter actually.

Limbo. Here o means opening or window - thus limbo is a place where people reach out the window - a prison.

Limber. A limb in err (limb be err). One's limb errs by bending too easily.

Lotion. Lo, t ion. A healthy fluid. "Lo, it makes firm the flesh".

Mad. One who may de. Apt to destroy. Man a de.

Madder. Means red - mad err is red in result - bloody. (Also gets red in face.)

Magian. Mag meant to magnify a thought picture. They had a mechanism for this in general use - a magian was one expert in the art.

Magic. The science of magnification of images. An electrical science like a very advanced television. The continued use of these indestructible mechanisms which they left behind them in the caverns is the source of our magic legends through the centuries. Merlin had a cave full of such mech in the Merlin legends of Arthur's court.

Magician. A magic an. One who knows magic.

Magnet. The net of force around a magnet. The mag part means it can be used to focus and magnify as in our electronic microscope. It is odd the ancients called a magnet an augmenting net if they did not know of such devices.

Magnetic. The science of such devices. Ic is always science.

Mail. May ill. Combined they mean "I'd better wear it, somebody might be ill". Anger was always ill, an illness.

Manacle. Lee from man act (man ac lee). To chain the man so a lee is formed from his hand's threat.

Mansion. A very illuminating word - man's ion. Place where a man has charged a sphere or chamber with beneficial electric.

Matter. A mixture of materials - a matt of err. Most stone and earth is a mixture of materials, unrelated but by accident.

Mean. A me an. An animal only conscious of himself.

Meander. To wander in a way that costs needed energy.

Medical. Me dic al. I know all detrimental things. One who has a remedy for most all de results.

Medicate. The ate means medicine to take by mouth.

Medicine. A medicine to take some other way - as a hypodermic.

Melodious. Same meaning as lady - me lower de for us.

Minikin. In is inserted into the word man to mean a diminutive being. The kin would mean active - active little fellow of almost microscopic size.

Morbid. More be I de. I don't want to be any more - I want to die. I deplore existence. (Note deplore.)

Mucid. M for man, u for you, c for see, i forI, and de for harm. "Man you see, I harm". Slime from a wound.

Negro - Negress - actually means a friendly slave (ro). A friendly helpful fellow - ne complementary attraction. Still the typical character of healthy Negros.

Neutral. Ne you t ral. Attracted by the charm (ne) of both parties.

Node. One of the important words. It meant place where no de exists - a life focii. Node is a focus of growth force, a nuclei of growth, an n from a good life.

Nun. Literally, sterile. Nu n. No seed.

Nude. Clothes are to protect from de. To be nude was to be at the mercy of de, but why the n is there I don't know except that nude and n go together. Perhaps new and nu are the same word and newly exposed to de was the meaning.

Nomad. Harmless person.

Obscene. O meant orifice, the source of life. Thus obscene is not hard to explain.

Obsolete. Out of use (oh be sol te). The sun renders useless.

Obsession. A little study of ess in this word will reveal a concern all of us have with it, even to the point of obsession.

Obovate. Egg shaped. (oh, be ovate.)

Ocean. See the source of life.

Odium. To give off impulse to harm. To hate.

Oculist. Here o and c mean orifice of sight.

Ogle. The impulse to gen begins with the eye.

Onion. On means on. Here the source (o) of seed (n) means continuation and on is a basic word formed from source and seed. An onion is a plant with a strong ionizing influence when eaten. It continues to overcome all other things eaten in its influence - in fact an on ion.

Optics. Science of vision - here o means eye.

Pace. The power of the an was measured in steps.

Pact. An empowered act. A binding act by power.

Panorama. P power, a an, o orifice, ra ray, and the ma probably the user, who was called a "ray". Power an meant a great mech operated by a ray. Thus a panorama is seen by use of a great ra of power.

Pane. A glass for a window, now. Then it meant the screen on which a panorama was seen by use of a ray.

Pate. The place where the power that holds men together is made. The unifying influence of thought - its home. Thus patriot derives from pate.

Peal. Power and *all* combine to give a loud sound.

Pedant. A walking ant (see use of ant in errant and arrant). Ped came to mean feet because power is usually signified by a lot of feet coming down - as marching troops. Thus p is power and down is de and coupled they came to mean feet.

Penal. Pen all - the all pen. Today the bull pen.

Pencil. Here pen is a writing tool. Pen can be an enclosure and a writing tool. A pen that sees ill is a good pen to write with

Pendent. Shape like a pen which hangs down? Or an imprisoning pit?

Peril. Power errs ill. That's peril, all right.

Pert. Power of attraction to an err degree (too much).

Philter. Ter - too great love - is accomplished by filling somebody with something. A love potion.

Plant. Plan t. The growing together of elements into a shape.

Planet. An e plant - here e inserted gives the impression that e was their all concept. Often e meant exd - the basic stuff from which all matter grows. The product of disintegrance whose reintegration is the source of all matter; thus planet is an exd plant, a growth in space.

while plant is any growth.

Pith. Power of growth in the human. The essence of man.

Plutocracy. A significant word: from Pluto, the ruler of the under-world in the time of the latter Gods. The race (family) from Pluto's realm rules. His methods of rule are still understood inherently in the use of the word.

Pond. Power on descent (the down meaning of de) means a mill pond - power from fall of water.

Potion. Power of te ion. A good medicine.

Prison. Price on. To hold for ransom.

Progeny. To generate the power of ro. To have progeny was to give birth to many children to work for you.

Prostitution. The p and the ro means they are controlled robots to a p ray. A p ray being one which overcomes the will by superim-posing a stronger flow of similar electric to that which is released by the cells in bodily movement. Thus prostitution is the illegal use of robots against their will by use of a p ray from a distance. Ro were often voluntary slaves as their system of society required it, and their lot was not necessarily undesirable. Thus Rome was a beautiful ro-bot city of the ancient time, and was so called because of its beauty: "O, ro me, too, it is so beautiful here", was the ancient meaning of the word ROME. Its government was primarily controlled by ray of the people, thus Rome - the city of robots.

Prostrate. A p ro lying straight.

Prototype. P ro to type. A standard form of man, unchanging.

Puberty. Er t. The time of greatest attraction between sexes.

Queen. Quest you energy seed. A bee queen is an insatiable appetite for birth - fecund for the whole ant hill. Thus que*an* is a low woman while que*en* is a high woman.

Quill. Quest you ill. Same meaning as pencil.

Quit. Quest you one te. Get someone else to do you good.

Race. Here the use of ray to mean a long continuation of anything is seen. Ra and line are the same word, often.

Radial. Ray d all. All lines from center outward.

Radius. D is always repellant - thus a ra d is outward - and radius is the spoke of the circle.

Radiation. Outward flow of t ions.

Radiator. Outward flow of *tor* or exd. Tor seems to have meant exd.

Rail. A bar to ill - to keep ill out.

Rape. Ra an p. Attack.

Rapier. A long sword - a ray of power - in its sense of a line an extension.

Rapture. Ray p te your e. A power ray attracts your energy, makes you healthy - thus rapture was the state their highly developed rays threw them into.

Ration. Ray t ion. They were entitled to a certain amount of beneficial ray treatment - their ration of ray.

Rational. One who believes in everyone getting some rapture from beneficial and stimulative rays. Rational still means the same thing today.

Recede. To fall back before a new discovery of detrimental flow.

Recent. Sent anew.

Recur. To see err (ur) and return on course - to return.

Reduce. To lower (d) again.

Reflux. Flux is flow - to reflow.

Reflect. Flec means to throw off lightly, thus reflect is to return in same path. Flect or flec should be remembered - as in flick.

Reflection. Occurrence of thought due to reflection of thought from a source in a mind reading ray beam - thus reflection is to see another's thought by its reflection in your head. Much of supposed original thought is reflected thought from others.

Repression. To hold back an ion flow in the brain.

Resolve. Sol is used in its meaning of taking things apart. Resolve is thus to analyze.

Scald. S (sun), c (see), al (all) d. S is used for burn - the sis sound. Badly burnt - all burnt.

School. S for the influence of dis flows and cool for the process of teaching which eliminates the err which they engender in thought. Thus a school is where hot-heads are cooled by teaching. The h is human.

Self. The s elf. The part of one's consciousness that mistakenly thinks s flows are thought. Thus the sun ro thought is called an s elf. Not our meaning for self - but the false self which counsels evil. Thus selfish is a survival of the original meaning of self.

Sesspool. S for decomposing and ess for cloaca. Also spelled cess pool - same meaning.

Sex. Same meaning as lady - one who combats the influence of sun. X for combat - s for sun influence.

Sin. Burning (s) and (in) for the cells or inner life of the body.

Thus sin is burning within the bod· and the mental destructive impulse which arises from such burning. Same as berserk.

Sinuate. Sinuous - as a flame.

Smash. S in its sense of taking apart - dis.

Solder. Hot stuff - it ders as sol (the sun) does.

Soldier. One subject to sol's command to destroy.

Son. A boy who will be a soldier.

Sorcerer. Sore and sor mean the same - a sorcerer is a conjurer who is always sore. A bad magician - a sorehead magician.

Sorceress. Same thing - only female.

Sororicide. The murderer of his sister (sorority?)

Sot. A sot is a drunk that sits still.

Speller. This word was a label. The word was followed by a question mark meaning - do you err in spelling? - use me.

Sphere. Sun power here - a burning sphere - a word for sun which came to be used for any round thing.

Spider. Spy from der. An evil sounding name for an evil insect - a der spy. Came from calling the insect by the most repugnant of person's names. One who worked for evil men by spying on good people to their destruction - a spider.

Spit. Here s seems to signify only the outward motion of dis - none of its other qualities mentioned.

Squib. A small fire-work

Stale. An old tale - here the age thought is meant by s.

Star. Most of the stars we see are suns; are burning. Thus we have s and t in a condition of ar - about to burn. Note that tar is inflamable matter. The use of *ar* to indicate this condition is frequent - thus roar is robot to ar.

Stake. A stick sharpened in fire.

Sterile. Ster is opposite of ter. A reason not to love.

Strife. Rife with burning. Combat is seen to mean in this case to be caused wholly by sun force.

Styptic. A burning tipped pencil.

Suicide. S you I see d. I disapprove.

Sullen. Was probably sol-len as in solemn. One who thinks somebody else should be burnt - as one is solemn when pronouncing a death sentence or counciling murder.

Sunstroke. The sun does not shine evenly; sometimes it gives off powerful groups of rays. The cause of sunstroke as rays from a sunspot.

Syllogism. Way of reasoning by which sun err can be avoided.

Tab. Count. Integrate animal be.

Tabid. Count one ill. One is sick. Take stock of sick ones.

Taboo. Prohibited for a good reason. Boo is same meaning used by kids when hollering Boo.

Tacit. T act I see. Understood.

Tact. A te act.

Talmud. Tale of earth (mu) disasters; (d) or *don't*s for laws. The book of laws for earth. M may mean man, and d -law.

Tar. A sailor or one apt to fight.

Tartarus. Hell. Our T is subject to ar; fire.

Tart. Combustile here means a substance burns the mouth.

Tenacious. Here the t means grip of t, ac act. Note how the sense changes from in tact - an attractive act - to tenacious a gripping act.

Terror. Here ter - love for someone, is in danger. Roar - the sound has lost its a but is still roar.

Thanks. Attractive human. I thank you - an k. I bless you with.

Thane. A th an.

Tether. A strong (t) tie rope.

Tot. Attractive little ot (zero). Almost nothing.

Tote. Negro in origin. The t meaning is evidently same as in ton.

Traction. Track of t ion. Act of drawing to one. To grip magnetically.

Tour. To err - travel aimlessly.

Toxical. Use of x with t means deadly. Poison.

Trope. Speech which changes the sense of a word. A p tero was a man eloquent - hence trope is power of tro.

Triton. Here Titan and tri for three pronged spear are combined to mean a titan with three pronged spear - which was a sea symbol. A fish spear. A sea titan.

Tufa. Fa is the old short for fallacious - is often used - thus tufa is lighter than it looks. Porous rock.

Tyro. A ro who doesn't know his work; is tied. A motionless worker. A beginner.

Uberty. Abundance. Note ber - too much (er) and be (b). T and y are a common use - meaning why do you t (attract) me with too much? Literally: you give me too much.

Udder. You de der. Good for one.

Ulcer. U (you) l (life) c (see) er (err)—Your life sees err. A sore. Cl seems often to mean far off - beyond. Thus ulster is a long coat. Ululate - a far carrying cry.

Ulna. Here na means bone, thus narwhal is a whale with a big bone on its nose; and natatory to help to swim. Thus ulna is a bone which helps to swim far.

Um. The reverse of mu. Seems to mean under - as umbriferous is shade, and umbrella a rain shade.

Un. Reverse of nu. The reverse of being born. To come undone. These words are I think from another language of that time - the language of opposites—thus Evil spelled backward means live; pit spelled backward means tip.

Undertaxed. If untaxed is all right why is undertaxed not enough taxed? The addition of der is significant here.

Unable. Un an be lee. Animal without a lee.

Unconcerned. Un and con combine to make unobserved.

Uterus. Womb and uterine - belonging to womb. Note the use of ter.

Utter. Extreme - wholly attracted.

Utopian. Ideal, uttermost possible development of an.

Uxorious. Foolishly fond of a wife. Note the addition of x and o to uter.

Valiant. Here val is in its correct use - v for vi or vital and all - all-vital. Thus a valiant.

Valor. Rich in val - or for ore.

Value. This vital energy of man life they used to indicate that a thing was of value. As valuable as life. Life value - as work-hours.

Vandal. Van in the front dal destroys all. One in the forefront of destructive action. Note how n takes the place of l, and the sense of beginning inherent in n (or seed or child) is used to indicate the front of a flow of people - the n of a mob is the vandal. A significant pair of words revealing their methods of making words.

Van. The front of an army.

Vanish. To go into s. To appear consumed by fire.

Vari. The combination of vi and ar means turbulent vital force - or varying growth.

Vegetable. Ve (vital energy); ge (generates) table. A plant that grows things for table. Note veg is just growth of life.

Venerial. Vital n seed err I all. Sexual life.

Venerate. To revere. These words were the same in their language, or almost the same.

Vernal. Vi err n, all. I love all, when young. Of youth.

Vernility. Note addition of ill in subordination of young sense of word to indicate servility.

Vibrate. Vital *be ra te.* Thus a vibration is a beneficial ray to them. Used for those vibrants which are beneficial, being rich in e (exd).

Voluptuous. Vol (will) up tu. To will up a strong attraction. Volupte - the ous makes it plural - or many voluptes.

Volute. Literally graceful holding - to will to hold.

Wade. Way of de. To walk down (in the water).

Wand. A rod to punish (will an de).

Wane. A rod to e (will an e).

Weird. We err de - of detrimental beings.

Woe. Woo energy? Are they kidding?

Woman. Whether woman is from woe man or woo man you figure out.

Xanthic. The yellow color of the sun is here indicated by its destructive nature to man. Xan - thic is thick yellow.

Xanthin. Yellow coloring matter.

Yap. Why does an p? P here means why does it activate its mouth.

Yearn. Yes, the n ars me. I wish to love.

Yeoman. Yes orifice man. Source of yes.

Yew. Yea *will.* A tough plant.

Yule. Lee here means a day of rest (why you lee). Get out of the wind and cold. A day for that, Yule.

Zeal. Ze means to be equal parts te and de, to zeal is to reduce to meaninglessness. Thus zeal is foolish ardor for an illogical cause.

Zero. One who is ro to meaningless forces. Came to mean nothing. A zero is one who works to create uselessness.

Ziz-zag The z meaning is here apparent as diversions from a course which are of no value in getting there.

Zooid. Inferior animal.

Zoo Collection of inferior animals of a useless nature.

Zoologist. Log is record - the recording person of a zoo.

WHY THE CAVES ARE SECRET

Richard S Shaver

The

HIDDEN WORLD

Spring, 1961

WHY
THE CAVES
ARE SECRET

By Richard S. Shaver

During the years there has been a heated argument about the location of the dero and the tero. I have said repeatedly where they are, but it has been the one point upon which my whole contention is hung which has been used against me, to "disprove" the whole thing. Scientific "fact", they say, cannot be argued against, and one single fact shatters the truth of my story to shreds. This one fact is the "hot" interior of the earth. They tell me that the interior of the earth is molten metal, that the "cold" skin is so thin, compared to the whole, that it is like a very thin-skinned orange. They say the skin of the earth is about 50 miles thick, making solid rock occupy only 100 miles in a total diameter of 4000. Thus, the area in which my caves can occur is only an area of one-fortieth of the whole. And here also, they say, this is greatly reduced because the lowest forty miles of this is, although not molten, at least red hot, and far too hot to support life. More, they say that this red hot rock is "fluidic" under its tremendous pressure, and any "caves" would automatically flow shut, and such a thing as a hollow place in such rock would be impossible.

They point out a "law" which says that temperature rises a degree for every hundred feet we descend into the earth. Thus, with a surface temperature of 70 degrees, we can go down only 7000 feet and we have a temperature of 140 degrees, at which point human life is impossible. Because I have placed some of my caves forty miles deep, and some of them *hundreds* of miles deep, they have "exploded" my whole position.

They are scientists. They *should* know. But let me use their *own* science. Say these wonder-minds: The earth's specific gravity is just slightly higher than that of water!

If the earth is composed of molten *metal* core some 3900 miles in diameter, I respectfully submit that it is a metal of *less* specific gravity than the metal these scientists say this core is composed of —*iron,* in the main. They say the metals at the *core,* the last hundred miles or so, are incredibly heavy, such as uranium. They are hoist by their own petard, for the specific gravity of the earth in its *entirety* admits only of a core of *water,* or something *no more dense.*

Can you conceive of "molten" water? Or *compressible* water, so that it is a "denser" water? These scientists have also said water is *not* compressible. They are, it seems to me, inextricably stuck in the mire of their own postulates, and *cannot possibly* claim my caverns do not exist, if they intend to mire them in their own mental muck!

I am not a scientist. (Even though I can prove, by published works in *Amazing Stories* years ago, that I have postulated scientific theories so correctly that the famous Albert Einstein said exactly the same things *years later!* His unified field theory: explained by me, in all its detail, in my exdisintegrance theory. Not only this, but *hundreds* of other theories—received from cavern records—which I can and *will* reproduce for you before I am through, with dates and comparisons with the work of *later* science. Most recent is the discovery that cosmic rays and radioactive radiation may be the *real* cause of the phenomenon of *old age.*) I repeat, I am not a scientist. And because I am not, these things which I have published in the past apparently point to some source of information other than my own *education* and my own *experiment*—both of which can easily be proved to have been inadequate to account for the results. I have said this source of information is thought records from the caves, played back to me by friendly tero; and actual conversation with tero.

So, not being a scientist, I repeat, with the most positive finality, the caverns *do* exist, and they are incredibly extensive, so that the possible population (were not so many dead!) could be *thousands* of times that of the *surface* of the earth, because it consists of so very many tiers of caves. The dero and the tero live in these caves. The caves are connected by broad tunnel highways, carved through the solid rock for thousands of miles, the whole inner earth being a vastly complicated network of tunnels connecting literally thousands of great caves as large as any surface city, and some so large as to dwarf a New York to insignificance.

Many of these caves are *filled with water,* having sprung leaks after thousands of years of being abandoned and uncared-for. But still enough exist, in which inhabitants do live, to be quite a sizeable population. Earthquakes have caused faults which have sealed some of the connecting tunnels. Other tunnels have collapsed roofs, filling them with rubble past which it is impossible to go. Thus, various settlements of dero and tero are isolated things, although enough tunnels exist so that it is possible to go anywhere from one place to another, if only by devious routes.

For those who still wish to argue with me on the basis of molten rock, and place the caves somewhere else, I will make a certain amount of concession, because it is a *reasonable* possibility. But I will stick to one thing, they *are* caves and tunnels! I have *seen* them with my own eyes, (or should I say with my mind's eye, because what is seen or sensed over telaug (augmented telepathy) is not exactly seen with the eye, but one *cannot tell the difference,* so it is legitimately "seen"—just as you *see* TV, yet nothing is *actually there* to see, only an "image". Telaug is the same (it can be sound alone, or sound and picture) except that it is far more vivid and real. Thus, I have seen that they *are* caves. Completely surrounded by solid rock. The tunnels *are* tunnels in rock. I have never seen any rockier rock!

If *you* want to say these caves and tunnels are not under our feet, but over our heads, in a sort of "another dimension" of this world of ours, perhaps you may be right! But nonetheless, it is a *part* of this earth of ours, of *this* planet. I have read of a conclave of mathematical scientists who have decided the earth does indeed have a "fourth dimension" and that phenomena exist in it! If the scientists can theorize thus, more credit to them. But it *proves* nothing, as yet. Until a better explanation comes along, I will maintain my present position of caverns under our feet, in the solid earth, and the devil take the molten core! for it does not exist.

Consider! If this earth were such a vast molten ball, the conductivity of rock is such that heat would be conducted *directly* to the surface in such copious amounts that the surface *also* would be red hot. Can you conceive of a molten metal "orange" with a *cold* skin! Even an asbestos skin! And, haven't you heard of the deep oil wells where the oil is so cold, and accompanied by salt water, that the pipes *freeze* as the oil is conducted upward, and must be melted with live steam! So it is a constant that temperature drops a degree each hundred feet, as you go down? Not so! Investigation of just a few mines will prove to you temperature is a very hap-hazard thing in the earth. So, I respectfully submit that you cannot explain away my caves by anything so unsupported by actual fact!

Now, where do most of the dero live? Mostly in caverns *close* to cities. Wherever you find a large city, you also find a settlement of dero. Why this should be so always puzzled me, unless there was contact with the surface—and I found out there was! The dero get much, if not all, of their supplies from the surface, particularly food. Meat especially. And what meat some of it is! J. Edgar Hoover tells us of the more than 120,000 Americans who turn up missing every year, and are never heard from again. I tell you that I have seen some of these Americans, hanging on hooks in the meatmarkets of the dero! Horrible? Yes indeed, indescribably horrible. Yet it is true.

But the dero also get clothing, tools, conveyances from the surface. How many Fords there are being driven along dark and dismal tunnels far beneath the surface of earth, would surprise you. And how many truckloads of supplies go into the wide doors of an innocent-looking warehouse in the center of a large city—and never come out again!—would also surprise you. Elevators to sub basements are such innocent things. Sometimes even a building inspector could not inspect sufficiently to discover that they actually go down to even lower levels! Nor would he have reason to suspect that this was so, and take the enormously difficult and costly steps to dig to find out! (And become "meat" in some market as a reward for his discovery.)

Dero also live in caverns not under cities, and *most* of the tero (those who are not detrimentally inclined) live under open country. One reason I myself live on a farm!

What do the dero do?

What would *you* do?—if you were incredibly stupid, with your mind deranged by powerful augmented radioactive rays constantly beamed upon you by ray projectors originally intended to beam beneficial rays, but now perverted in their activity by being sun-polared—the rays they manufacture are detrimentally radioactive-infected, and the rays they conduct from the surface are multiplied in their poisons by the machines so that they are far more damaging than they are to us surface people.

You would find yourself in possession of many marvelous machines left by the Elder races, and you would use them in idle childish play. You would use the telaug and vision rays to spy upon surface people, and you would use the projection rays to fool them with fantastic images, you would use the tractor rays to open railroad switches before speeding trains, you would even be so childish as to trip people going down stairs, open manhole covers before them, and so on. You would use the marvelous surgical rays for the diabolical slicing of delicate nerves in the brain, or other parts of the body, to create mental and physical cripples. You would burst their hearts so that a "heart attack" would eliminate some important person and cause chaos in surface governments .You would do an almost fantastic number of things that could add up to the veritable "works of the devil"!

Except for one thing: you would risk retaliation from tero at equally powerful ray mechanisms, a sort of "balance of power". But occasionally, as some guard suffers a momentary lapse of vigilance, or has his attention diverted, you will be able to get in some quick deviltry, and you will howl with sadistic mirth at the result.

For you are mad! Madness in the caves is an almost universal condition. It cannot be otherwise, for more than one reason. First is the reason that you are exposed to ray damage much more extensive than is caused normally by the sun (and the moon—you've heard of the madness caused by Luna's rays, not a myth, and a superstition, but based on fact, for Luna's rays are only sun rays, polarized by reflection, and thus dangerous to a small extent). Moonlight and sunlight, conducted upon the dero cavern dweller by his augmenting apparatus, subject him to much more detrimental effect than on the surface.

The second reason is that the human mind (and the dero are as human as you and I) cannot stand too much torture without cracking; and torture is a part of the daily life of a dero. Few indeed have not at one time or another fallen into the power of a mad local despot and been subjected to unimaginable tortures besides which the Inquisition's devices are child's play.

A third reason, perhaps more effective, though more insidious, is the extensive and perverted use of the machine called "stim". The ancient purpose of this machine was to accentuate the pleasure derived from sex, largely by beneficial rays which restored energy as fast as it was dispensed; and also was a health machine, dispensing various nutrients and vitamins and minerals directly through the skin and into the body. The dero spend days at a time in these machines, indulging in an orgy of sex that, rather than being stimulating, is exhausting and detrimental because the stim machines are contaminated by radioactives and their good effects nullified and turned instead to bad effects. Because of them, recessive elements of heredity are accentuated, and a continual downward genetic scale is the result.

Yet, in madness there is craft! Incredible craft, and it is coupled with great secrecy. These degenerates aren't going to risk the pleasures that are theirs, by letting any surface people take them from them by force. Interlopers are slain (after torture), and secrecy is maintained at all costs. Because of the aid their machines give their mental processes, this craftiness is vastly multiplied, and it would take a clever surface man indeed to out-think them in the direction of subterfuge, etc. A vast curtain of error is continually hung before the eyes of surface man to conceal the truth of their existence. And it is an incredibly effective curtain. It is the most insidious propaganda imaginable, and involves hypnotic effects hard to believe. *Was* that thought you just thought, your own! You would be absolutely certain it was yours, if you were certain there was no way for anyone else to think it for you. And it takes a great deal of experience to be able to see a thought for an alien thought, when it occurs in your mind. But it can be done. Question your thoughts with reason sometime, and see if many of them are not thoughts that would not have occurred to you in the natural reasonable course of thinking. Question your dreams sometime. The effects of hap-hazard stringing together by your subconscious of your own personal, and sometimes long-forgotten memories? Ever have an incident in a dream come from something beyond your memory—honestly? Something you *know* isn't anything you remember, because never before experienced?

Subtlety is here. And if entirely unsuspected, totally effective.

But to admit such things to a psychiatrist is to admit to mental derangement. To admit them is to risk admission to an insane asylum. So, here on the surface, the secrecy pattern is maintained, even by surface people. You yourself, if you hear a voice, can be and usually are, your own worst enemy!

How did I learn about caves? I've said it before. At first by an inadvertent contact, because I seemed to be "in the know". Then by contact with friendly tero, who, because I had accidentally gotten in on the secret, and seemed friendly, and harmless, and did maintain the secrecy, was allowed snatches of information and contacts that led to more contacts. Then some real tero friends who began to pass on to me knowledge that might make man a better man, and happier, just as they have for countless ages, sneaking bits of knowledge to men whom we revere today as the "discoverers" of great scientific principles. Nikola Tesla was such a man. Edison was such a man. Investigate for yourself the "mystic" overtones of each man's life! Read Edison's diary, and see how close he was to the borderline of admitting he heard voices, and that there were strange "psyche" sources for much of his knowledge. Read how Tesla invented things by simply "copying them" from actual visible and functioning projections hanging in the air before him! So it was with me, and they showed me much.

But then I broke the secrecy rule, and thereafter fled across the world, pursued by vengeful dero, sometimes protected, and sometimes not—and the "sometimes nots" have mostly destroyed any chance I've had to accomplish what I intended. Even my story was perverted into fiction, until it was subject to ridicule.

Proof? You want proof? Having read this far, is it reasonable for you to *demand* proof? Not very. Yet, there is proof. Everywhere you look! And I'll try to point those proofs out to you. Let me just speak my mind, with no regard to coherence or continuity, so that somewhere in the hodgepodge, you may seize upon some ammunition for thought, so that you may start thinking for yourself—the proof will appear, as effective proof as is possible to give.

You will see that I *can* "hand you" a machine! Machines you use every day. But you will ask that I hand you a "new" machine. Perhaps I *can*. Perhaps I shall! It has been said: "ask and ye shall receive." Exactly that has been known to occur before! Remember you any of these incidents? *Recognized* you any! Oh was it God who answered your prayer! Or somebody else's prayer? But you *have* observed it! Do you *remember* it!

TO those who cannot accept my work as anything but misguided imagination, or who think the whole "Shaver Mystery" is a rather stupid hoax the following words are to be considered exactly that: more stupid contributions from a man who is purposely hoaxing stupid readers into believing silly things that could not possibly be true. To "Police Psychiatrist," I fearfully apologize for suggesting they might be wrong, and that a George Murmans might exist outside a man's head as well as inside. I apologize to position power and solemnly swear that nothing said here is to be considered as anything but a rather stupid hoax which some readers enjoy being fooled into accepting. To "Public Official" I also apologize for suggesting he knows more than he might publicly admit of such things, and solemnly swear that this is all untrue and he does not have to worry about it at all.

To you gentlemen who are intrigued by this "Hoax," I can only say you will find very interesting data here, and that such people as professors of colleges, psychiatrists and policemen, mayors and insurance investigators have to be allowed their foibles, and we can disregard the necessity for considering them sane quite as much as they can disregard (and do) the need for considering us the same.

FIRST, clarifying is in order. Letters in large numbers have accused me of implying this and meaning that—which I didn't. The confusion arises of course from the fictional treatment my message has had to be given.

Some readers have drawn quite a variety of erroneous ideas. Some of them are right. The truth is wild enough to suit anybody. But I wish to get the picture clearer for them.

One of the commonest errors is in the use the word "dero" has been receiving. Readers infer in their letters that all cavern people are "deros", and "dero" and "cavern dwellers" are synonymous. That is wrong! We wouldn't be alive if a large part of the people down there weren't fighting like hell for us and for themselves against the true "dero".

A dero is a cavern wight whose ancestors had the habit of bringing in the sunlight over the penetrays. Their evil nature is due to a constant "hearing" (telepathic) of sun vibrants because those same penetrays they use to bring in the sunlight and warmth were designed to handle thought-waves, to detect and augment waves of those frequencies heard by the brain. Their brains got dis (infections) on the lipoid films of the brain cells, where thought is generated. This went on for centuries, for an age, and the hereditary result was a dero, the ancient "Devil" of mythology, and his people —humans whose minds handle only disintegrant pattern thought. ALL CAVERN PEOPLE ARE NOT DEROS, thank God.

The good ones do a lot of work for us, in subtle unseen ways, avoid tamper accidents by helping out a driver, get some doctor info on how to stop a plague, and are the source of some of our modern inventions by handing over suggestions to an inventor, unbeknownst, because they saw a similar device in the wreckage of the caves.

Even all the bad ones are not deros. A dero is an automaton of evil, and not an ordinary crook. He isn't that smart.

I would like, too, to state clearly and simply and generally the main themes I was trying to get across in my fictional work.

I am trying to say that our civilization is a sham! That our education is a very shoddy substitute for what it could be if the truth of our past were known.

I am trying to say that if we knew who and what some of our present-day bosses really were, we would be vastly worried at their apparent careless and oppressive attitude toward ourselves, the people—which attitude is shown in their deliberate deprivation of all science of the advantages that would arise from a general knowledge of and study of the rays and mech with which their rule is enforced.

They hold that they won't turn over the info, that it is like an atom bomb in importance, and they are keeping it in their own hands.

I reply that I wish they would, because so many deros use it, too—and that they don't need to keep the *whole* of that science a secret. So much of it is purely benevolent and medicinal. Truth is, they are not educated, do not realize what they are doing in keeping the whole a secret still today.

I am saying there are millions of people besides Shaver who know there are vast caverns under earth, full of strange, miraculously potent machinery—and that they do not speak because it is so obvious that they would be misunderstood to the point of persecution.

I am saying that if our scientists were ALLOWED to have but one of these machines (which exist in great profusion and in fine repair) for study, that our whole technical development would be accelerated beyond imagination. I am saying that some of our modern developments are due to information about the Elder race methods that filter through the age-old "iron curtain" between the deluded surface races of man and the undeluded but oppressed races under our feet.

Man's age-old persecutors, the "Gods," the degenerate debauchers, the secretive age-old monopolizers responsible for these delusions we have and call history; the persecutors we have and claim do not exist; the condition of war and misery our races are in, *once exposed* would not, perhaps be so terribly harmful to him, would find a remedy.

I am saying that the people responsible for filtering through to us some of the technical secrets which find their way into our modern technologists' brains are due to friends among these hidden people, and that these friends in the underworld are the only members of that strange society that a sane modern man can consider as also sane.

The rest would be beneath our attention except that they *can* destroy us with the ancient mech (and do, regularly, kill many,) debauch us with the ancient wonderful stim mech, and craze us with the detrimental rays of that forgotten science.

I AM trying to show that it is possible and probable that there *have been* members of that society in the past who lived for centuries beyond the normal life span—as legend tells us. That they did so because of the nature of the ben-rays and canned nutrients still to be found in the sealed storerooms.

That there probably *were* rulers who lived for centuries, and that some of the most repressive and reactionary of the present-day rulers of the cavern groups *MAY* have been alive for two or more centuries.

That the medieval minds, cruel and vindictive and vandalistic, are so because they are still in a medieval state of development socially, and *they were raised that way.*

That these secretive, reactionary, sadistic minds among them are today holding back the whole race of man from ALL true development. That they are striving with might and main to place all human life under a rule of malignance unimaginable, that is so horrible in its aims, in its degenerate cruelties, so destructive in its details of government that the race of man will perish if they succeed!

And *you* insist they do not exist — want an "artifact". (Can you get hold of an atom bomb to swap for the "artifact-mech"? It's a deal!)

I am trying to say that the enlightened ones among them who struggle against this goal need our help if we can give it—and that we can't if we insist they *do not exist!*

There are many things I have heard that I do *not know* are facts. To mention these along with the things I know *are* facts causes an almost unavoidable confusion.

I have heard that surface light and power and coal are possessions of the ray-people. I don't *know* it, I *heard* it. I have *heard* that some of them have harems of thousands of young women. I don't *know* it. I DO KNOW they have harems, and an oriental contempt for all western morality—but because of the nature of social life developed around the use of stim-rays, I can understand this different morality.

I KNOW many terrible things that I cannot find a way to tell except as fiction. These are things so lurid and impossible they are hard to make credible even in a lurid stf. tale. They could not be considered as facts by an ordinary man, because he has not seen and could not accept. These are looked for by those who know something of the great secret, and look for recognizable information in the "forbidden" field.

I KNOW they have weapon rays that kill at fifty miles and more. That they *hit* what they shoot at with these. A man cannot even think of such weapons without fear; still we must—and *they have been with us* right along.

I KNOW they have telaug beams that hear thought from a man's mind up to fifty miles and more. That is an extremely sensitive receiver, for the sending of one brain is not exactly powerful in voltage.

I KNOW they visit space, and receive visiting ships from space, some of which do not get away again. I don't know *why* they return to earth, for *no one here* is getting a square deal! The ships that return must belong to those who *think* they benefit from the repressive throttling monopoly of all the good things of earth.

I am saying that earth's peoples are supporting a destructive, extravagantly luxurious and decadent "secret class" who rob us of our birth right—the science that could be learned from the mechanisms of the Elder race; which same mechanisms are the instruments that have held this class in power for many, many centuries.

I am saying that, due to many conditions which we cannot understand over a long period of time, many of these people are idiotic, and unfit to be allowed to continue as our "secret" overlords.

I say that if people generally knew this condition, they would lose the awe and fear that keeps from the race of man many great secrets which would prove a new and greater path of life for all of us.

I am saying to these men who cry "we want an artifact, an inscription, an ancient mss, we want proof!"—you *have* proof all about you! But your minds are so slanted by wrong teachings that you misinterpret these artifacts and remnants on the surface which tell the truth about the God cavern's existence.

Egyptian hieroglyphs, Mayan temple drawings, innumerable such sources are chock-full of references to the caverns, but since the science which interprets these relics has no word for any of these "myths" except as myths, that is how they are interpreted—as childish tales only.

Only by going into the caves and returning with the actual pieces of mechanism could these gentlemen be convinced. If *any* of the thing is true, any logician can know *that* is an *impossible request*. It is like sending an Ambassador to Russia in a top hat and frock coat, striped pants and brief case, and asking him to bring back proof that the Russians are contemplating a world revolution. He would be turned aside everywhere he went, and would come back with what we already know (if he came back at all—which is improbable)—"the Russians have an iron curtain on information."

I don't blame the Russians overmuch. But I *do* blame the cavern people because so much of the cavern mech is *medical* in *nature*. It would revolutionize all medicine if M.D.'s had penetrays; electric needle rays for surgery without incision; beneficial rays that can keep a dying man alive long, long after he would ordinarily die; beneficial rays that make a man think several times as well. Their science was based on a knowledge of man's nature far beyond our own—and nearly every one of their mechanisms is of some immediate physical use to health!

So we are deprived of them because they keep some idiot in wealth and power, who does not even know enough to have technicians hired to study and develop a knowledge of the nature and uses of these machines. Who has no real grasp of the importance of the caves!

YOU ask for proofs of the giganticism of the far past—and *you* can find Devil's Tower (Wyoming) in any Atlas. It is a national monument! If it isn't a gigantic petrified stump larger than any redwood ever hoped to be, I will eat my hat! The stump alone is taller than the Empire State building! What size were men when trees grew that size?

THEY were the men who are spoken of as the Aesir, under Ygdrasil's branches, planning a battle against the Frost Giants! And they had telaug beams (Odin's Eye), and they had "magical" underground dwarfs, and icy underworld realms of magic—and *we* have only the Devil's Tower to prove it today. But it was a long time ago; when the sun itself was more beneficial and less aging. BUT BROTHER, HOW CAN YOU ASK FOR PROOF WHEN YOU HAVE A DEVIL'S TOWER?

Through our dope rings (now don't tell me there are *no* dope rings) daily many men and women are sent to the underworld. What becomes of them? They don't come back? No! They become slaves or worse. In some cases they are employees; but at the mercy of a capricious despotic class who kill for pleasure. One might as well be a slave.

These people leave no traces! Did you ever try to trace a man to a dope den? You can't. It has "protection", and it is *not* a dope den. Don't tell me you don't understand. How could I prove a certain place was a dope den, and that people disappear there regularly? You know even the F. B. I. has a hard job with these things, never get them all. I don't think they even *touch* a ray-graft; because it is an old "taboo", and they know better than to try. I *think* they leave it strictly alone.

We don't know *how* the secrecy is maintained. I *do* know that it *is,* and that the things I say go on, *do happen.*

But I could no more *prove* many such things than I could prove that Standard Oil cheated on their income tax. Nor could anyone.

But there *is* a vast number of eye-witness testimony; there is a vast amount of writing from the past that is misunderstood; there is a mass of incontrovertible proof—IF YOU INTERPRET IT CORRECTLY! But you don't! You say the old standard explanations over and over—and they are part of the curtain that has been erected for an age between common people and the Forbidden Fruit.

For the Forbidden Fruit is the greatest pleasure on earth; and from our present day standards or morals, it is an immoral pleasure. Hence it remains hidden—although the truth is it would be the greatest stimulation our form of society could receive. Men would develop—for it would furnish a vast incentive to science and invention and medicine (especially) that is now lacking!

As I see it, what the two classes, the two "worlds", need most is a mutual port of trade, a city or a market or a place where the things of value from one world may be openly traded for those of the other. For our washing machines we would get telaugs and stim mech and small levitators and similar apparatus which would be infinitely valuable to us—and from what I have seen, *they* could use the washing machines, yes!

Secrecy has acted as such a throttling thing on their life that they cook on stoves Ben Franklin would have called obsolete; sit on wooden benches; slave in child labor factories; are two hundred years behind us socially. Many of their pieces of furniture (brought in in past, much of cavern needs furnishing) would bring a fortune as Victorian and pre-Victorian antiques. (Not speaking of Elder race antiques.) For, since the days of telegraph and newspapers and radio, the secrecy has required an almost total lack of commerce or intercourse between the worlds. (Before the days of newspapers, there was commerce.)

And it *is* a world, the Elder World, and *it* does contain wonders in the still working ancient mechanisms, but it also contains the most brutally reactionary minds on earth; as well as the most modern and liberal minds in certain groups.

They can't have radios, because radio can be traced. (Many freighters had to give up radio when crossing enemy waters, as the radios rebroadcast a wave that can be detected.)

They can't have clean modern markets full of good food from America's canning factories—the commerce necessary to fill them would cancel their "secrecy". Thus this reactionary policy from the past is just as disliked and as unpopular among them as it would be among us if we knew it existed. Thus such enterprising men as myself have backing more valuable among them than among the surface people. Truth is, I have more friends among the cavern people than on the surface, and far more valuable ones.

They want the ancient barrier to the full development of their life removed, too, just as much as "we who know" on the surface want it removed. They want the sweatshops made humane down there, they want better living conditions, better sun camps where they can take their rays on the surface without worrying about watching eyes. They want less restrictions on their life, and the "secrecy" custom is the most irritating and harmful of all their restrictions.

Such things as Hecate, the bloodsucker, will exist among them in the future, if the science monopoly continues. Such things have plagued their lives in the past when the great ben-mech rays were more potent than today. The rays and the superior nutrients found in the storerooms of the Elders kept them alive much too long—and they were evil. But we do not *think* we have any immortal Hecates today.

BUT, TODAY, we *do* have a parasitic (class of) creature battening upon us, who has developed a technique of parasitism as highly evolved as a vampire bat's, and as ingrown in his nature! This is the "reactionary" behind the "secret" monopoly of the antique Elder weapons and pleasure mechs—and *he* is the enemy we seek to expose. *He* is the enemy I would die to harm in any way; to wrest but one of the mighty Elder secrets from *his* unworthy and unusing hand. I would die cheerfully for the race of man. It was what I expected when the Shaver Mystery series began; but I found there were more of the cavern peoples in my way of thinking than I had expected. Publicity was its own protection.

For *he* deprives *them* quite as much as *he* does *us,* and it rankles them much more because they are fully conscious of *his* cost while we are ignorant even of *his* existence. We do not see the young girls go into *his* harems; we do not see their wrecked bodies later. We do not know of *his* awful abuses of the rights of man or see the tortures and battles in *his* game arenas; do not see the human pieces in *his* "Bickro" games. (Human chess to the death.)

But *they do know* all these horrible things and they want the course of decadence changed and reversed as much as myself. So it is that we try to give you what you naively call "proofs", it is like a blind man trying to ask a man with eyes to prove that he sees.

ONE either "knows" of the underworld or one does not. It is very much like a seeing race with eyes living beside and among a race without eyes who refuse their existence. BUT WE ARE PRESENT AND WE DO SEE! (*We* meaning those on the surface "who know".)

But for a man who doesn't care to go out and question pimps and prostitutes, criminals and dope peddlers, yeggs and assassins; who doesn't care to pore over newspaper and police files for strange and unexplainable occurrences, or Missing Persons lists for data on the losses to the underworld; for a man who would like something more than eye-witness accounts from the lips of such "unreliable" humans; who doesn't care to question the personnel and inmates of an insane asylum on "what the voices say" (which I will admit could develop into an embarrassing expedition) there *is* a simple method of proving to himself that the Underworld (in the Classic sense of the word UNDERWORLD) does exist in all its miraculously preserved wondermech, building on building and boring on boring, city bowl on city bowl and city tier on city tier—deep in the earth—peopled with a citizenry of diverse and numerous skills in using the ancient mech to cause miracle and devilment.

This method is in the application of the Shaver alphabet to the English language and indulging the deductive faculties in tracing the words of the Elder tongue which still can be found, many times in a good state of preservation, in our own English language.

Those college products who have been endowed with a complete knowedge of the past history of every word by etymololgical wizards of the colleges, by those professors who *assume* that the past students of the evolution of languages have all been correct in *their* assumptions, and have carefully grafted all this *hoary paraphenalia of error* upon their students; those gentlemen are the men who have the greatest difficulty in finding any sense in this alphabet.

They cannot successfully make the mental adjustment necessary to a study of the alphabet, because they cannot, even for the sake of experiment, admit for one moment that it "could be possible". So they glance at it and throw it aside because it was not on the curriculum at college and hence can be of no possible importance on this green earth.

Nevertheless by its use the basic meaning sounds of an ancient ancestral tongue can be traced by any student flexible-minded enough to make that initial allowance for a base from which to proceed.

These basic sounds, such as RA TE DE AN BE CE FE GEN ENG I KIN LO LEE LI MA MU MO NIN NE O SIS TEAT ST UND VI VE VIE VIT WIN WER TER DER XE Y ZE and RO can be found in so many words meaning the same thing, in so many languages meaning the same thing, that we get a picture of basic sound meanings that we can trace back and back to a once universal tongue. Gradually to a student this once universal tongue emerges as Mantong—and every word he says is translated by his mind into its Mantong meaning, which is a greater meaning.

It cannot be done by utilizing any system of word derivation now taught; for they are false, and it did *not* happen that way! If it did happen as they say it did, it happened *long after* the word had come into use over the whole earth, and their assumptions of its adoption into use and its spread are consequently error because they mistake in a given language an already existent word for a later derivation from some other word in some other language.

It wasn't that way. They only had a common universal source in one ancient tongue. If they did derive from two or more Elder sources, they still intermingled during the great lapse of time to form a mixture inextricable today because of their original similarity in concept-symbol or basic-sound meanings.

This *point of departure* on the study of ancient tongues forms an insurmountable barrier between the classical student and myself. He cannot admit *to begin with* that there could be possible a basis for such an assumption that there *was* an original universal tongue.

He is confused by the multitude of his learnings. HE KNOWS the Egyptian came first, or the Coptic or some other irrelevant tongue and he knows that all similarities must be traced to original source of which he has already been informed. He presupposes himself into a state of admiration for his deduction which is only, after all, a complex assumption of firsts, derivatives, etc.

But, above all their squabbling over each word, Mantong emerges as the great Rosetta stone of the past. Touch any tongue with it and the veils fall away; the Mantong stands clear and clean above it all.

NO OTHER tongue contains their knowledge of energy, or gives a key to their wisdom—a wisdom greater than our own—and any student proceeding from an assumption that this wisdom never existed cannot proceed even experimentally in the study of the tongue.

For it is based on the play of two forces, and all phenomena of life are described as an interplay between these two forces De and Te, evil and good, Dis and Int.

Ssstt describes the touching of fire to water, of water to a hot stone—to us as to any primitive. BUT to a student of Mantong *sssst* is the survival of the ancient symbol of sun-fire, for dis striking against the ancient symbol for TE, for growth. The water contains the TE or growth force, and when it comes in contact with S, the fire, the noise *ssstt* always comes with it—and they used the symbols of these two primal forces with the sound which they make.

De was their sound symbol for the processes of disintegrant energy. *De vi* was their word for an evil man's energy. *De vile* their word for one filled with *de; de cay, Dee See a* (animal) *Y*.

Decay is a *sentence* in Mantong. It means: *see dee in the animal,*

WHY? It *taught*. When the child learned the word decay, he learned to look for the *cause* of the *decay*, too. Hence the letter Y (why) is tacked on so many of their words. But no classical product of our colleges would ever admit that such a system of word building ever existed for he cannot admit that anyone in the past knew that much!

Add a little more detrimental disintegrant en-energy—we get DE AD. *Dead* meant: if you keep adding de you will die. You can't even monkey with the stuff (as we are learning with atom bombs —and are going to learn really by losing all our "precious" civilization in one flaming battle).

Dead also meant: someone had killed a *DE unit* of the social pattern. Their words had these coincident punning meanings packed in! De a De! A command to go out and make likewise any Hitlers or would-be Hitlers was inherent in their word for a dead person.

The word *teat* we cannot even say without lewd and comic thoughts. They meant something more; they meant: *TE force is here at teat.* (The child absorbs integrative energy here.)

Get a college word wizard to admit that any first race on earth ever knew of any such thing about energy as that there were two basic forces, integrative and disintegrative! It isn't even taught yet (or is it?) that there *is* an integrative force that disintegration demands an equivalent integration or there wouldn't be anything to disintegrate in all space. OUR COLLEGES DO NOT TEACH AN INTE-GRATIVE FORCE (to my knowledge), or even suggest that it could be a pole about which all life proceeds upon its beginnings until it meets DE and ceases to BE!

How then get them to admit that the ancients knew there was an integrative force and used it as a basic symbol for GOOD, for a way of life in the word TIC, even though the word tic itself describes our present world system of finance and commerce. They called it TIC—we call it Credit. But they meant a lot more by TIC than we do by the word *credit*. They meant a social order based upon credits—we call it money and we get it for work. Credit—(See RED, I T.) Our own word is one of theirs: "I will stand T for your RED (ink)." We still get in the "RED." We think it is modern slang for the red ink used on losses columns, but in truth they used the word before there was ink. Before Carters ever made a bottle of red ink for bookkeepers to itemize their bills with men used the words "in the red" to describe their debts.

We all have these unconscious assumptions in our minds about words, and most of them are wrong.

I can go on and on with this, but I don't want to tire you. BUT if you *are* interested in a proof of the Shaver mystery, it can be had by any deductive mind for a few hours work with the alphabet, and the Mantong of the Elder race will emerge in all its wonderfully simple meanings before him, and he will have a complex and wonderful plaything for his mind in its idle moments all his life. For every word bears some flavor of their thought, if you can search it out. And it isn't so hard as our complexly misinformed professors would have us believe. Because they *are* wrong about the past, and there *is* better history in *King Arthur* and *Merlin,* in *Froissart's Roland and Oliver,* in fairy tales and myths than there is in any standard text on Classical history on "Rome and Her Fall", on the "Rise of Athens". Those histories *are* correct *as far as they gc;* but they *missed* the *true beginnings.* We did *not* begin with the pyramids, the way the history books do! We *had* a vaster beginning than any Pharaoh's foolish piling of block on block to provide a place to put his mummy. And a much more intelligent beginning. To me, the Pyramids are not a *great mystery;* they are a sample of the imbecility of men in certain early periods AFTER THE FALL. That the cumbrous piling of those square children's blocks of stone into a pyramid had a meaning, a vast significance, or any other fol-de-rol that is taught about them is not my way of thinking. They are sheer imbecility made concrete, and we still pretend to ourselves that the Egyptians who built them had "wisdom". The *wisdom* they are talking about existed *long before* the pyramids, the latter priests who *understood* that wisdom had nothing whatever to do with causing the pyramids to be built.

Wrap all the mists of wool about a pyramid that you want. I still see a fool making a million lives painful that he may have a hole to be placed in when he dies. PWA on a grand scale in ancient Egypt; a fool king who wasted the lives of his people upon idiocy.

THE Elder race *had wisdom.* Some of it *can* be found in the basic sound-meanings of our tongue by use of the Shaver alphabet. I do not claim to have "originated" the alphabet. (To *me* it *was* a discovery. Others may have done so.) Maybe I *heard* it with "voices". Whatever is the truth, it will discover to you a vast race, prove their existence on earth, and give you an inkling of their mighty thought-rays.

I could go on talking about the Elder language for a large book-full, but there is no space for that. Eventually it will (the book) be done, if not by me, by some one like yourself who has read me and understood there was more to the Shaver alphabet than meets a college know-it-all's eye.

About proofs of the Shaver mystery, it is so self-evident to one who talks to ray people over rays from their caverns every day, it is somewhat like asking an ordinary householder to prove the Electric Light Co. exists.

It is *not* evident to you who have *not* "heard voices", "seen ghosts", experienced what are called "illusions due to mental derangement", but which we who know call "projections", or "telesolidographs".

It is like two men living near the same river. One has never seen a fish in that river all his life. The other has caught fish in the river every day. They get into an argument, the one who believes there are *no fish* in the river says: "Show me the proof, the bones and tails, the heads of these fish you have caught."

Well I will show you what is left of some of the fish I have caught in the river of sound that flows from the cavern world to those who are allowed to hear. *Snatches of conversation heard over ray:* "GOES UP—IS COMING!"

The words mean nothing to you; *to me* they tell that the ancient plan of coming to the surface and ruling openly is again being taken out of the closet and being brushed off for a new trial. Perhaps *"they"* will come out and rule with antique-ray openly, and all of us will see it in our lifetime. It is a thing that has been planned many times, fell through because of fear, difficulties of moving apparatus, disorganization due to their medieval governmental set-up, etc.

"— — — — — WAS DOWN HERE. HE WAS THE TOUGHEST MAYOR IN TOWN."

The words mean our surface Mayor — — — — — — was down in the caverns on a visit, and that he was seemingly the "toughest" of the group of big-shots with him, of the underworld characters whom he visited. One does not *know* if he really *was* down there, we only *hear* the *words.*

"TELL, 'EM OUTRIGHT, SHAVER, GET 'EM DOWN HERE? WE NEED 'EM PLENTY!"

It means that there are plenty of the people down there hoping and praying that some effort like my own does break through the dense cloud of "modern" ignorance in America and gets some action out of our powerful nation before less worthy rulers than our own Republicans and Democrats take over—both up on the surface and down in the caverns. But they themselves find no way of telling the men of the U. S. that will be understood, believed and acted upon. When they do talk to a man, he is frightened, thinks he is having delusions, goes to a psychiatrist and has himself psycho-analyzed. There is no greater ignorance, no greater barrier to progress than the blindness engendered by the sense of all-knowing self-sufficient egoistic fol-de-rol our educational system has given our average American school product.

I love those people down there, fighting unseen and unheard and unhonored, fighting and warding off from *us* a fate that words cannot describe. The dero of the caverns could depopulate the earth within months if they were free to do so, with the antique mech-rays. These people are ignored by our "omniscient" statesmen, though many of them *know* much of the caverns and their secrecy, and we *could* help them much if only the curtain of "it isn't true", "they don't exist", "voices are imagination" were gone.

That is what I am trying to do; remove that curtain once and for all. Believe me, it is vitally necessary or I would not have the courage to face the possible consequences!

"HAND ME SOME DRY NEEDLES!"

Meaningless phrase isn't it? But not if you *see* the torturer, his needles slippery with blood, reaching for less elusive tools.

It *would* be possible to *buy* some of the mech in *certain parts* of the cavern world. These locations where the caverns are peopled by humans with some idea of developing a *future* for man could be found—*if* the whole governmental and "scientific" set-up of the nation, of the world, were not too "smart" to be taken in by such a "hoax". Hex doctors, other practitioners of the black art such as Demonist cults, *do buy* apparatus from the underworld! Not the men who DON'T "hear voices" (even when they *do*). Statistics show that *everyone* hears voices sometimes—not the scientists who call everyone who does not agree with them "crack-pots"; not the gentlemen who have learned all there is to know about life, the interior of the earth, science *and* Einstein. You yourself, if you are honest with yourself, must admit that you have "heard voices" at one time or another in your life. *Think carefully.* AH! You had put it aside as imagination! But *was it?* No. *it wasn't!* It happened!

MANY things could be obtained of infinite value from these people in the caverns, if all of our civilization was aware and trying to salvage even a bit of the mighty wisdom the Elder race left behind them in their miracles of machine art. BUT it *can't* be done as long as "officialdumb" frowns upon all such efforts as *"superstition"*, "black art", or "crackpots". It is a vital and unseen side of our life WHICH MUST BE OPENED TO THE PUBLIC GAZE!

The fact is that any honest investigation of super-normal manifestation *always* and *invariably* turns up *mighty important data;* which data is *shelved* by fearful, ignorant and bigoted people who are *quite sure* that the school books are *right,* and that they *cannot* go contrary to opinion or they will lose their "position".

You see in today's paper: "THREE AIRPLANES DISAPPEAR COMPLETELY WITH FOURTEEN MEN IN THEIR CREWS." You see, *every day,* a constant succession of such Fortean occurrences, such impossible accidents and wrecks and catastrophes. On our "fool-proof" railways the signals go awry and one part of a *famous* "cross-continent flyer" runs into another part —of *the same train! Over and over you read of the "impossible" happening!*

Yet you are told there are *no* caverns, there *could not be* any "antique miracle machinery", AND I MYSELF AM TO BELIEVE THAT I AM THE VICTIM OF DELUSIONS. EVEN THOUGH I HAVE FELT THE SEARING RAYS, BEEN TORMENTED BY INVISIBLE DEVICES, SEEN IMPOSSIBLE PROJECTIONS OF THINGS THAT DO NOT EXIST ON EARTH TODAY AND TALKED TO THE PEOPLE WHO MANIPULATE AND USE THESE DEVICES EVERY DAY AND HAVE BEEN DOWN THERE AND SEEN AND TOUCHED IT ALL WITH MY OWN HANDS.

It would be *comforting* to feel that I *was* the victim of a self-deluding mental quirk, for I would realize there was *no* threat hanging over the heads of the American people; there was no *need* to overcome the blindness of these people, that *no deros* kill regularly and steadily by such methods as caused Heirens to kill for George Murmans. That if I did not try to do what I do, these killings such as Suzanne Degnan would not be in part upon my head. For I know that much could be done to stop such killings if only people *knew what the real cause was.* Locking Heirens up did *not stop George*

Murmans. George Murmans can *kill you!* It would be smarter to punish the psychiatrists who deny George Murmans exists, for they probably *know quite well* that the voices *have* real people behind them, and are not *men enough to admit* that all is *not* understood about such phenomena. A psychiatrist is a worse criminal, *if he does* know, a *greater coward than Heirens* seems to be, blaming it on a phantom.

Every experienced psychiatrist *has heard hundreds* of people *confess* they "hear voices", and that some of the "voices" *prompt them to criminal acts.* Yet how many have the courage to *affirm* the voices' real existence. THEY ARE AFRAID OF YOU, the public! Yes, they *fear* the *common man's conviction* that "all such phenomena are delusions" and, *that fear is justified!* BUT, SOMEONE, SOMETIME, HAS TO CONQUER THAT BLIND DENIAL OF FACT AND COME OUT IN THE OPEN WITH THE TRUTH ABOUT VOICES, ABOUT SUCH CRIMES AS HEIRENS', AND ABOUT SUCH THINGS AS AVOIDABLE TRAIN WRECKS.

It *must be faced.* All right, we face it, and thousands of readers flock to our support with letters affirming our decision to attempt the heretofore impossible!

Here's hoping we succeed. For there *are* in the caverns such things as weather machines, set in a pattern to govern the whole continent, that can control the precipitation, the winds, the whole character of the weather. I have seen them operated, have *touched* the machines; but *how do I tell it?* I have as much trepidation about the attempt as Heirens. He (can you blame him?) flunked the test of courage. I face it. (Remember this is a "hoax" please.)

THESE machines, of infinite variety, are culled over by engineers from rival (underworld) countries such as England (for all we know) and what is not sold to them is wrecked by the destructive nomads of the caves "so someone else won't use them".

Gypsies *"know"* about the underworld. Spiritualists insist on the reality of their *"spirits".* I know the gypsies are making better sense about the voices than the Spiritualists. They tell fortunes by allowing the secret rays to read their customers' mind—and make money. So do the spiritualists, but they *say* it is spirits. The gypsies *say* it is a *"gift".* It is! From "gypsies" under the earth. BUT NOT DEAD! DID YOU EVER ASK THE WEATHERMAN WHAT

BECAME OF THE RAIN THAT STARTED RAINING AND SUDDENLY QUIT, AGAINST ALL PROBABILITY? DID YOU EVER ASK A PRISON GUARD HOW COME CERTAIN GUARDS SHOT AND KILLED OTHER GUARDS? DID YOU EVER ASK THE MISSING PERSONS BUREAU WHERE ALL THE PEOPLE WENT? PERSON-ALLY (not by listening to the radio—but personally looked at the files comprehensively)? Did you ever talk to insurance investigators who ascertain the cause of fires, the nature of the mechanical failures in train wrecks, all the many things that go unaccountably wrong?

NO, YOU DID NOT! You *assume* there was nothing mysterious or frighteningly weird about any of it. YOU ASSUME THAT IT IS ALL PERFECTLY UNDERSTOOD BECAUSE OF THE NATURE OF YOUR EDUCATION.

Fact is, a black witch doctor in Africa does know more about such things than *you* do. They don't close their eyes to all the unseeable things in life. But a "modern professor" *does* so close his eyes, and succeeds in closing most of his students' eyes.

All of which wouldn't matter, if most of our heritage in the caverns wasn't being destroyed and wasted and broken by idiotic handling by creatures with no wits or education whatever. It *matters* because our civilization *could receive* from just one piece of that "mech" a bigger boost than from many generations of genius. BECAUSE THAT MECH IS THE PRODUCT OF AGES OF INTENSELY CIVILIZED DEVELOPMENT BY A BIGGER, GREATER RACE, A RACE WHO HAD CONTACT WITH SPACE!

How to tell the American government there *is* something to learn about the rocks of mother Earth that *can't be learned in a College of Geology,* in an "Institute of Mining Techniques"? *How* to tell a modern over-educated bigot that our school text-books left out the biggest page—the history of the Elder race? HOW?

It can't be done! The answer tells me to give up, to write stories about anything else, to quit making dangerous statements about a people who might take umbrage and bump me with some of that wonder-weapon-mech.

Then a voice says: "Tell 'em but right! Be a man!"

THE SHAVER MYSTERY—15 YEARS IN THE MAKING

THE WHOLE TRUTH AT LAST — AND NOTHING BUT THE TRUTH!

No one could have foretold, when it was first published, what a sensational reaction there would be, and to what it would lead. Nobody could have said it would disturb millions of people the world over, and make a permanent mark in Man's thinking. Even the great Albert Einstein was to be challenged (and successfully as events have proved!) to say nothing of the sciences of physics, astronomy, and the philosophical sciences of metaphysics and mysticism. Now, after 15 years, the Shaver Mystery stands in a unique position, a pivotal point in modern philosophy, possibly the answer to most of the enigmas of all times.

What is the Shaver Mystery? There are many theories. There are those who support Shaver in his materialistic honeycomb of caverns the world over, heritage of a Titan-Atlan race which fled a poisoned world over 12,000 years ago. There are those who call his caverns the "astral", his dero the spirits of the dead. Some say it is "another dimension", another realm of life alongside ours, invisible under ordinary circumstances. They fight among themselves, but in one way they join solidly together—the Shaver phenomena are REAL, no matter how opinion of their nature varies! Here is a mystery that stretches from the madhouse to the White House; from the moronic to the world's greatest minds; from superstition to scientific knowledge; from the forgotten past to the present instant!

www.ingramcontent.com/pod-product-compliance
Lightning Source LLC
Chambersburg PA
CBHW061759250726
48657CB00001B/196